Historic Tales
of
FLAGSTAFF

Historic Tales
of
FLAGSTAFF

KEVIN SCHINDLER & MICHAEL KITT

THE
History
PRESS

Published by The History Press
Charleston, SC
www.historypress.com

Copyright © 2019 by Kevin Schindler and Michael Kitt
All rights reserved

First published 2019

Manufactured in the United States

ISBN: 9781467142410

Library of Congress Control Number: 2019940045

We are honored to dedicate this book to the memory of two longstanding pillars of the Flagstaff community, Richard Mangum and Randy Wilson. Though we lost them both in 2018, their legacies live on.

CONTENTS

CONTENTS

PREFACE

Sometime around 2001, I, the senior author, accepted an invitation from a Lowell Observatory colleague of mine, Mary Lou Evans, to attend a meeting of Flagstaff history enthusiasts. The group was known as the Flagstaff Corral of Westerners International, and they were a worldwide network of people interested in the history of the American West. I enjoyed watching the evening's presentation while meeting fellow history enthusiasts and, before I knew it, was elected "Sheriff" of the group with my wife, Gretchen, taking on the duties of "Deputy Sheriff." In these roles, we succeeded Dick and Sherry Mangum, Flagstaff historians who had published a number of books about the city and who had headed the Flagstaff Westerners for the previous decade.

Dick and Sherry, as well as the many lovely members, were quite welcoming and kind to Gretchen and me. We were excited to be a part of such an enthusiastic and friendly group, and we looked forward to running our first meeting. When the time came, we showed up early, got everything in place and began welcoming our guests. We enjoyed meeting many members for the first time, but we soon realized that we were short one vital guest—the evening's speaker. Gretchen and I huddled to discuss how we might proceed in a way that didn't result in us getting run out of town for failing at our first meeting. A lady standing nearby overheard our strained whispers and made her way over to us. "Honey," she said to me, "my mother was a Harvey Girl and I give programs about the Harvey Girls over in Winslow. Would you like me to step in and talk to the group?" I gushed a most enthusiastic "yes" to this angel, and she gave a remarkable and well-received program. And that was my first experience with Flagstaff history.

Within a short time of becoming sheriff, I again followed in Dick's shoes and took over writing a monthly history column for northern Arizona's *Mountain Living* magazine. After doing this for several years, I realized that these columns combined could make the basic outline for a book about Flagstaff history. This wouldn't be a comprehensive volume attempting to cover all aspects of this history, but it would be a collection of anecdotes that highlighted some of the people, places and events of Flagstaff's past.

This book idea percolated for years until 2018, when my friend Mike Kitt and I tossed around the idea of working on a book together. Over the years, Mike has written an observing guide about the moon and numerous columns for *Astronomy* magazine and a publication called the *Observer's Guide*. Mike and his wife, Karen, have a longtime interest in astronomy, and they have both been instrumental in the preservation of Lowell Observatory's storied history. They have devoted many hours volunteering at the observatory in this regard, and they have played a key role in creating the Putnam Collection Center, where the observatory's historical materials are now archived.

We initially discussed writing a book with an astronomy theme, but I remembered that Flagstaff history book I had thought about writing years before. Mike was naturally enthusiastic about switching to a history theme, and we jumped in, modifying some of the past columns while writing new content. A particular interest of Mike's is Northern Arizona University, an institution that has played a pivotal role in Flagstaff for more than 130 years, and the reader will see numerous references to it throughout this book. The result of our joint efforts is a gathering of stories, the topics biased to some degree by our particular interests. So many more stories are out there, and we hope this book not only stimulates conversation about Flagstaff's rich heritage, but that it also inspires other historians to share the tales they have tracked down.

Acknowledgements

$\mathcal{T}$his book has benefited from conversations throughout the years with generations of historians and others who are knowledgeable about some aspect of Flagstaff's past. Of particular note, and in no particular order, are Richard and Sherry Mangum, Eugene Hughes, Joan Brundage-Baker, Susan Olberding, Bill Lyons, Earl Slipher, Lisa Schnebly Heidinger, Kathy Farretta, Nikki Lober, Susan Longerbeam, Deb Harris, Joe Meehan, John DeGraff, John Westerlund, Malcolm Mackey, Bill Putnam, Henry Giclas, Donna Ashworth, Steve Verkamp, Susie Verkamp, Drew Barringer, Jerry Schaber, Jerry Snow, Mike Amundson, Vince Murray, Jim Turner, Steve and Lois Hirst, William Sheehan, Jim Babbitt, Rose Houk and Chris Scully. Discover Flagstaff staff members and volunteers (Heidi Hansen, Trace Ward, Lori Pappas, Joyce Lingenfelter, Meg Roederer, Ralph Schmid, Mike Russell, Candace Schipper, Delmy Payne, Jessica Young, Cherri Lamont, Carrie Nelson, Jennifer Schaber) and the members of the Flagstaff Corral of Westerners International.

Lauren Amundson (Lowell Observatory) and Cindy Summers (NAU's Cline Library Special Collections and Archives) helped track down several images, while Michael Collier provided several of his own outstanding photographs.

Jerry Snow, Susan Olberding, Joan Brundage-Baker, Jeff Hall, John Westerlund and Mary DeMuth read the manuscript and suggested edits that improved the readability and accuracy of the content.

Acknowledgements

Versions of many of these stories previously appeared in a variety of magazine and newspaper columns written by me, Kevin Schindler. These were all made possible by Seth Muller (*Mountain Living* magazine), Randy Wilson (*Arizona Daily Sun*) and Dave Eicher (*Astronomy* magazine).

Lindsey Givens and Ashley Hill of The History Press guided the development of this book and offered many suggestions for its improvement.

Many more people contributed to this project with their enthusiastic support. Special thanks to Bonnie Stevens, Florence McGuire, Allison Bair, Alma Ruiz-Velasco, Mary Lou Evans, Danielle Adams and Rich Bohner for their inspiration.

I appreciate the love and support from Gretchen, Alicia, Addie, Sommer, Brandon, Senna, Lauren, Mom, Donnie, Terry, Kim and their extended families.

Mike Kitt would also like to recognize all that his wife, Karen, does to make endeavors like this possible.

INTRODUCTION

Like many things encountered in life, history is a relative thing. The city of Flagstaff, for instance, was founded in the late 1800s. Boston, Massachusetts, is more than twice that age, and Paris, France, dates back a couple thousand years beyond that. So, things that are considered old in Flagstaff may seem pretty modern in Boston and Paris.

Yet the relative youth of Flagstaff doesn't mean it hasn't seen its fair share of fascinating history. Plus, so much of Flagstaff's identity is tied to its natural history, which dates much further back, and in some cases, predates human habitation. The volcanic mountain range known as the San Francisco Peaks and other nearby features, such as the Grand Canyon, Lava River Cave, Grand Falls and the old-fashioned stone used in construction nicknamed "Arizona Red" are considered characters in the story of Flagstaff, alongside the Babbitts, Henry Fountain Ashurst, Wilson Riles and other individuals.

Put these characters together, let time run its course and the result is an unlikely, and sometimes wacky, narrative that transcends the confines of a single western community. One such character was a young ranch boy who learned the power of speech at a young age and became one of Arizona's first congressmen, and he was so well-known in this capacity that he was cast in a Hollywood movie. Another character in Flagstaff's history was a man who not only built a beloved hotel and movie house, but who also built a folly of a road into the San Francisco Peaks. His road, during its short lifetime, allowed tourists to experience a Switzerland-like alpine setting and astronomers to reach for the heavens. A lesser-known name in Flagstaff lore is Philip Johnston, who built one of the community's early motorist hotels. However, he is more famously known as the father of the Navajo Code Talker program—the only spoken military code that was never deciphered.

A classic example of the mixing of characters and stories is Meteor Crater, a three-quarter-mile-diameter gouge in the earth north of Flagstaff. A piece of the space rock that created the hole thousands of years ago sat on display at the Grand Canyon for a century, which probably included the time that Theodore Roosevelt became the first sitting president to visit the Canyon and Arizona. The space rock was eventually moved to Lowell Observatory, the place where Clyde Tombaugh forever changed our view of space with his 1930 discovery of Pluto. Meteor Crater was a place described—and photographed—by aviator Charles Lindbergh, who, after he flew from New York to Paris in 1927, came through northern Arizona several times while helping to set up a transcontinental airline passenger service. Meteor Crater was also visited by the Apollo astronauts in preparation for their voyages to the Moon.

These people and these places are closely interwoven to create the tapestry of Flagstaff, which blankets and ties together the past and present.

Surveys Open Up the West

*T*he first non-Natives to see northern Arizona were likely members of a party led by Garcia Lopez de Cardenas that broke off from the main Coronado expedition of 1540. They were searching for the fabled Seven Cities of Cibola, but their search came up empty. Three centuries later, a detailed exploration of northern Arizona began with several expeditions that set the stage for eventual settlement.

The Treaty of Guadalupe Hidalgo, which ended the Mexican-American War of 1846 to 1848, resulted in the so-called Mexican secession. This resulted in the addition of land that comprises the present-day states of California, Nevada, Utah and most of Arizona, along with smaller portions of other states such as New Mexico. The geographies and natural resources of these lands were largely unknown, so U.S. government officials planned several expeditions to gather information about the area, with their primary goal being to establish transportation routes. Several of these campaigns traveled through northern Arizona. Captain Lorenzo Sitgreaves of the U.S. Army Corps of Topographical Engineers led the first expedition in 1851. Its goal was to explore the Zuni and Colorado Rivers in hopes of finding a navigable water route to California. While doing this, the group would also collect plants, rocks and animals in order to learn about the area's natural history.

The party left Santa Fe, New Mexico, in August and made several stops, including a three-week stay at the Zuni Pueblo. They left the Pueblo on September 24 and followed the Zuni River to the Little Colorado River.

On day fifteen, now in Arizona, the explorers halted as they arrived at a steep waterfall with a vertical drop exceeding that of Niagara Falls. Located around thirty miles northeast of Flagstaff, this feature would become known as Grand Falls, or Chocolate Falls to some locals, because of its muddy, brown water. While this discovery essentially extinguished any thoughts the party members may have had of using the waterway for regular transportation, later generations of explorers would realize a different kind of value the river and surrounding span of cinder cones and volcanic rock had—scientific. Geologists would study these features to learn about the inner workings of the earth, while astronauts, the explorers of other worlds, would train here in preparation for their voyages to the moon.

Following the advice of expedition guide Antoine Leroux, a well-known mountain man, the expedition left the Little Colorado River at Grand Falls and headed west toward the San Francisco Peaks with the idea of meeting up with the Colorado River near the Grand Canyon and then following its course. On the way to the Peaks, the expedition came across the Native American ruins at Wupatki, marking the first Euro-American record of the site. Several days later, the expedition stopped at a bubbling fount of water on the southwest side of the Peaks. Later named Leroux Spring, it became a critical water source for future travelers and, eventually, residents. Just west of the spring was a stretch of land later called Fort Valley. It was the future site of the U.S. Forest Service's first forest research facility. Physician Samuel Woodhouse was serving as the expedition naturalist, and he became the first person to carry out extensive scientific observations and collections in the area, which established the critical groundwork for later generations of explorers and scientists such as naturalist Clinton Hart Merriam. Four decades after the Sitgreaves Expedition, Merriam developed his now-classic life-zone study based on his observations of flora and fauna on and near the Peaks.

As Sitgreaves led his men across northern Arizona, immigrants from the eastern United States were trying to find their own way to California after they had been urged there by the 1848 discovery of gold at Sutter's Mill. The need for a reliable transportation route was now stronger than ever. Most interested parties realized that a railroad would be the best option, so Congress appropriated money to undertake several surveys to determine the best route. One of these was led by Lieutenant Amiel Weeks Whipple from 1853 to 1854 and traveled along the thirty-fifth parallel, which goes right through modern-day Flagstaff. The core of the expedition left Fort Smith, Arkansas, on July 14, 1853, and was later joined in Albuquerque by U.S.

Army First Lieutenant Joseph Christmas Ives, their guide, Antoine Leroux, and others. The expedition included approximately seventeen scientists, who made widespread collections and observations and significantly added to the knowledge of the area's natural history.

In Arizona, the party discovered remarkable samples of petrified wood in an area that was later designated as the Petrified Forest National Park. Later generations of scientists would exhaustively study these world-famous deposits, which include a rich sampling of dinosaur bones and other fossils. As the expedition neared Flagstaff, it stopped at a chasm that Whipple named Canyon Diablo. It also stopped at the archaeological site, Cosnino Caves, and nearby Turkey Tanks, which would prove to be a reliable water source for future travelers through the area. The group went to Leroux Spring, which later served as a base for the expedition when they would split into small groups to explore the area. These smaller excursions explored the land encompassing the present-day Museum of Northern Arizona. Little could those explorers know that that spread of land would one day serve as home to a museum dedicated to the study and preservation of the local natural history and culture that they were then exploring.

H. Balduin Mollhausen chromolithograph of Whipple Expedition campsite at Leroux Spring near base of San Francisco Peaks, 1853. *From "Diary of a Journey from the Mississippi to the Coasts of the Pacific with a United States Government Expedition," 1858.*

Modern sign indicating path of Beale Trail, which is located near Laws Spring west of Flagstaff. *Kevin Schindler's collection.*

The surveys conducted by Whipple and others indicated several feasible railroad routes, but politicians couldn't agree on one and ordered additional surveys. Until these could be completed, they authorized a wagon road that could temporarily serve travelers. They named navy Lieutenant Edward Fitzgerald Beale to head the project. Beale, known for contributing to the gold rush by carrying the first California gold samples across the country to the federal government, brought in more than fifty men and, famously, dozens of camels to build the road. Beginning in 1857, Beale and his crew traveled back and forth several times constructing and improving the road. Often following the trail created by Whipple, Beale's route passed by Cosnino Caves and Turkey Tanks to Leroux Spring and through modern-day Flagstaff on its way to California.

In 1857 and 1858, Joseph Christmas Ives led his own expedition to explore the Colorado River. He explored the river from its mouth to about where Hoover Dam is today, and he traveled east to explore the south rim of the Grand Canyon. This expedition produced the first illustrations, geological cross-section and map of the Grand Canyon. The group continued east through Leroux Spring and on to Fort Defiance.

The era of transportation surveys wound down in the late 1860s. In 1867 and 1868, a U.S. Army colonel, William Jackson Palmer, led an expedition through northern Arizona, following the path of Whipple and Beale, and he demonstrated, once and for all, the viability of a thirty-fifth-parallel route for the railroad. In his 1869 published report of the excursion, Palmer not only named Agassiz Peak, but he also used the term "Grand Canyon" in print for the first time.

These expeditions collectively impacted northern Arizona in several ways. They laid the groundwork for the arrival of the railroad, which resulted in the founding of Flagstaff in 1882. They also revealed the bounty of natural resources that led future pioneers to settle there and scientists to carry out their research.

A Mountain of Names

$\mathcal{M}$uch of Flagstaff history can be learned by studying the namesakes of various streets, facilities and natural features in the community. Milton Road, for instance, refers to the old lumber town of Mill Town, which is centered in the vicinity of today's Days Inn on West Route 66. There are also the majestic San Francisco Peaks, which stand sentinel over Flagstaff.

Less than a million years ago, a series of volcanic eruptions piled layers of lava and ash on top of each other to form the sixteen-thousand-feet-high San Francisco Mountain. Over the years, further eruptions, combined with normal weathering and erosion, caused it to collapse and wear down. This left a ring of smaller peaks with prominent summits surrounding an inner basin.

A common misconception is that the name of the Peaks came about because early settlers could see the city of San Francisco from the top. The term actually originated in 1629, 147 years before the city in California was founded. Franciscan friars established a mission at the Hopi village of Oraibi, seventy-five miles northeast of Flagstaff, and named the Peaks after the founder of their religious order, Saint Francis of Assisi.

Native cultures in the region held the mountain in high esteem for its religious significance. The Navajo people recognized it as the westernmost of their four sacred mountains—along with Mt. Taylor in New Mexico and Colorado's Hesperus and Blanca Peaks—and called it *Dook'o'oosłííd*, which in one translation means, "the summit which never melts." Hopis used the name *Nuva'tukya'ovi* ("place of snow on the very top") for the mountain. They

The San Francisco Peaks as seen from the northeast. *Kevin Schindler's collection.*

saw it as the home of their sacred kachina spirits and used it as a reference point for determining the winter solstice, which marks the renewal of life with a new planting season.

As for the main peaks making up the mountain, the tallest (12,633 feet) is Humphreys Peak, named by geologist Grove Karl Gilbert in 1873 after Andrew Humphreys. As a major general in the U.S. Army, Humphreys oversaw the survey records collected by early exploration expeditions through northern Arizona and eventually became chief of the Army Corps of Topographical Engineers, but he never saw the peak named in his honor.

Perhaps the most well-known of the peaks is Agassiz, the only other 12,000-foot summit (12,356 feet) in Arizona. It is often mistaken as the tallest of the peaks since it blocks the view of Humphreys from Flagstaff. It is the center of Flagstaff's downhill skiing industry and is where the Arizona Snowbowl is located. The Snowbowl's name dates back to 1938, when a contest was held to name the new attraction. The final list included names such as Frosty Run, Hopi Heights, Alta Vista, Winter Haven, Lolomai and Pahoki, but the eventual winner was the more prosaic Snowbowl.

The San Francisco Peaks as seen from downtown Flagstaff. *Kevin Schindler's collection.*

The namesake of Agassiz Peak—Louis Agassiz—is commonly known, but the story behind the man and his family is perhaps not. Jean Louis Rodolphe Agassiz was born in Switzerland in 1807. As was common for many nineteenth-century naturalists, he was educated in the medical profession and trained to be a physician. He spent his career, however, as a zoologist and geologist. He studied fossil fish early on, but he later turned his focus to glaciation. His revolutionary ideas on this topic made him famous around the world.

In 1846, he was invited by John A. Lowell of Boston's Lowell Institute to lecture at the institute and become a professor at Harvard. The Lowell Institute was founded in 1836 as an educational foundation that offered free public lectures about various scientific, social and religious issues. Its founder, John Lowell Jr., was the great-uncle of Percival Lowell, who founded his own observatory in Flagstaff in 1894, a dozen miles away from Agassiz Peak. Agassiz accepted John Lowell's offer and moved to Massachusetts, where he helped found Harvard University's Museum of Comparative Zoology and became one of America's first influential scientists.

During William Palmer's 1867–68 expedition, he led a group into the western territories along the thirty-fifth parallel to survey for a potential railroad route. He named Agassiz Peak after Louis Agassiz, since he had classified many of the fossils collected on the trip. Palmer intended for the entire San Francisco Mountain to be renamed as Mount Agassiz, but other people used the name specifically for the second-highest peak of the mountain.

Agassiz was also the name of a short-lived community established in the Fort Valley area, eight miles northwest of downtown Flagstaff. When a group of homesteaders from the East Coast, the so-called "first Boston party," came to the region in May 1876, they laid out a town site and named it Agassiz after the great scientist. Due to poor weather and lack of mineral resources in the mountains, the party abandoned the site within a month. Speaking of name origins, during a celebration of the country's first centennial on July 4, 1876, town members raised a flagpole, which later led to the naming of Flagstaff.

Agassiz's son, Alexander, was also an important American scientist who spent much of his career associated with Harvard. Alexander's son, George, was a good friend of Percival Lowell's and gave him a telescope that Lowell Observatory still owns today. George visited Lowell many times in Flagstaff and enjoyed telescope viewing in the shadows of the peak named after his grandfather.

As for the names of the other peaks, Fremont Peak derives its name from soldier and explorer John Frémont. He earned the nickname "Pathfinder" after leading several expeditions to the west in the 1840s and 1850s. His provocative tales of adventure inspired many Americans to travel west. He also served as a soldier in the Mexican-American and Civil Wars, ran for the office of the president in 1856 as the first Republican to do so and served as the governor of the Arizona Territory for several years.

While Fremont, Agassiz and Humphreys peaks were named after people who lived outside of Flagstaff, the other principal peaks of San Francisco Mountain all derive their names from locals. Museum of Northern Arizona founder Harold Colton named Doyle Peak in 1933 in honor of local legend Allen Doyle, who was one of Flagstaff's early pioneers. This brings up the case of confusion over the true identity of Doyle Peak, which is historically described as the ridge located between Agassiz and Fremont Peaks. At one point the name was erroneously used to describe another peak—Schultz, which is the rounded one a bit lower and to the right of the more angular peaks, as seen from downtown Flagstaff—and confusion has persisted ever since. In any event, Allen Doyle moved to the area in 1881 and initially worked as a cattle rancher. He later built a trail to the top of the San Francisco Peaks and the first road for automobiles that connected Flagstaff and the Grand Canyon. Perhaps most famously, Doyle guided luminaries, such as writer Zane Grey and Sharlot Hall, Arizona's first "state historian," around northern Arizona.

While the Doyle name is familiar around Flagstaff, the name Aubineau is less so, even though it is crucial to northern Arizona history. Julius Aubineau was a native Frenchman who moved to Flagstaff in 1891 and served as the town's mayor a few years later. He was critical in the development of the community's water system when he helped to create a pipeline that brought water from the peaks to the town. He was also responsible for building Flagstaff's first sewage system. For all of these contributions to the community, Aubineau Peak was named in his honor.

Another important Flagstaff resident who lent his name to one of the peaks was a teacher named Tom Rees. Moving from Ohio to Flagstaff for health reasons, Rees herded sheep for a time before going into public service as clerk of the Coconino County Board of Supervisors. He was later elected

Signpost along Humphrey's Trail in San Francisco Peaks. *Kevin Schindler's collection.*

as clerk of the Superior Court and became a popular and active member of the community. Rees held leadership roles in the Elks, Masons, the Boy Scout Council and his place of worship, the Federated Church.

The last of the peaks, Schultz, was named in honor of Charles H. Schulz. (For some reason, the "t" was added when naming the peak.) He was another early Flagstaff pioneer who arrived in 1880 and settled in the peaks to herd sheep. He eventually owned one of the larger—if not the largest—sheep herds in Arizona and also served on the Coconino County Board of Supervisors.

An old Japanese proverb states, "Tigers die and leave their skins; people die and leave their names." In Flagstaff, these names are further chiseled into history by their association with the names of the individual San Francisco Peaks.

THE BABBITTS

A popular tale in Flagstaff tells of how one of the area's hundreds of cinder cone volcanoes, located fourteen miles northeast of Flagstaff, got its name. It seems that a local rancher scaled the 820-foot-high peak sometime in the 1890s. From that vantage point, the rancher observed a four-mile-long black lava flow that had spilled from the volcano some seventy thousand years ago. To his eyes, the cratered cone and adjoining flow strongly resembled an old-fashioned, portable toilet, known as a chamber pot, that had fallen over and spilled its contents. Inspired, the rancher called the previously unnamed volcano Chamber Pot Crater, except he used a less refined word in place of "chamber." As schoolchildren might say, the four-letter word begins with an "s," ends with a "t" and is high in the middle. The name stuck with locals, but censor-conscious mapmakers refused to incorporate the questionable word and so shortened it to "SP Crater." What is surprising about the story is the identity of the rancher—a quiet, dignified man not known for such vulgar language. His name was Charles "C.J." Babbitt. He was a member of the legendary Babbitt family that came to northern Arizona in the late 1800s and developed a wide-ranging empire dominated by livestock and mercantile interests, as well as community service.

The Babbitt story, as it pertains to northern Arizona, began on a cold spring day in 1886, when businessman David Babbitt and his younger brother William stepped off the train in Flagstaff. They had been operating a business in Ohio with their brothers but got the itch to go west to find

Aerial view of SP Crater. *Michael Collier.*

their fortunes. David and William liked what they saw in Flagstaff and invested the brothers' $17,640 in ranchland and a small herd of cattle. To identify their stock, they created the CO Bar, in honor of their hometown of Cincinnati, Ohio. Several months later, their brother C.J. arrived, and by 1887, the fourth brother, George, had also moved to town. The last of the brothers, Edward, came in 1891 after finishing law school. They expanded and diversified their operations into a successful family enterprise that is still in existence today, and many Babbitts are still serving the community in a variety of ways. The cattle industry has remained a strong component of the Babbitt ventures, and through the years, they have purchased the Hashknife, Arizona Cattle Company and other cattle outfits. The Babbitts also thrived in other areas, such as operating trading posts, department stores, farms, mines, automobile dealerships, garages and an ice plant. At one point they took over operation of a funeral parlor, and someone soon came up with the line, "From the basket to the casket with Babbitt's."

David, born in 1858, was the oldest of the five brothers. In 1888, he opened a mercantile and housed it in a new building constructed of "Arizona Red" sandstone at the northwest corner of Aspen Avenue and San Francisco Street. This building, which has been modified several times through the years, still stands and is run in recent times by David's

The five Babbitt brothers: George, Charles, Edward, William and David. *Northern Arizona University, Cline Library, NAU General Photograph Collection.*

grandnephew James E. Babbitt as an outdoor gear shop. Aside from operating the mercantile, David dealt with many other aspects of the Babbitt operation. He also found time to serve as Flagstaff's first acting mayor in 1891, and he headed a committee that developed Flagstaff's early water works. He married Emma Verkamp, who had lived across from the Babbitt's store back in Cincinnati. Her father liked the Babbitt brothers and not only ended up being father-in-law to three of them, but he also supported them with both advice and money.

George Babbitt, born in 1860, was perhaps the most refined of the brothers. In addition to his business interests, he served as Coconino County treasurer and was one of three trustees who pushed for the construction of a reform school. He obtained the necessary funding and the building was erected, but Flagstaff residents didn't like the idea of such a facility in their town and eventually the idea was dropped. The building was instead incorporated into the Northern Arizona Normal School and was named Old Main. George served as a trustee at the school for several years.*

The third brother, William, was born in 1863, and he focused his energies on the livestock aspect of the Babbitt operation. A simple man, William seemed happiest when out on the range with cattle and cowboys.

C.J. Babbitt, born in 1865, married a Verkamp sister, Mary, and worked mostly as a stockman. He shocked his brothers in 1900 with a purchase that most cattlemen would have loathed. While riding on a trail north of town, C.J. came across a herd of sheep, and by the end of the night, he had done the unspeakable: he had purchased all five thousand sheep. The Babbitts thus entered the sheep business, which led to the quip, "Even the sheep say Baa-bitt." That same year, C.J. also built Flagstaff's first mansion, at the southeast corner of Cherry Avenue and Beaver Street. He lived there until 1910, when he moved to a less opulent house several blocks away. The mansion remained as a landmark until 1964, when fire destroyed it. A new building was constructed on the site, which in recent years has been occupied by the Theatrikos Theatre Company. Some of the large blocks of rock that marked the mansion's property remain. As for C.J., he was the longest-lived of the Babbitt brothers and passed away in 1956 at the age of ninety. Several of his progeny became well known for their participation in politics. His sons James and John served in the state senate, and his grandson, Paul, was elected mayor of Flagstaff and, later, Coconino County supervisor. Paul's brother, Bruce, served as Arizona attorney general, Arizona governor and United States secretary of the interior during Bill Clinton's presidency.

The youngest Babbitt brother, Edward, was born in 1868 and served as a lawyer in Flagstaff during his handful of years there. Before moving back to Cincinnati in 1896, he was elected probate judge for Coconino County and served in the Arizona legislature. He also married a Verkamp sister, Matilda. Though he lived in Flagstaff for just a short time, he significantly contributed to the community. With brothers David, George, William and C.J., he established the Babbitt empire in northern Arizona, which continues to thrive to this day.

A note about Northern Arizona University: The university has gone by several names through the years, including Northern Arizona Normal School (1899–1925), Northern Arizona State Teacher's College (1925–1929), Arizona State Teacher's College at Flagstaff (1929–1945), Arizona State College at Flagstaff (1945–1966) and Northern Arizona University (1966–present). Throughout this book, we use the name appropriate for the time.

HENRY FOUNTAIN ASHURST

*I*n an early scene of the 1962 movie *Advise and Consent*, Lafe Smith, played by Peter Lawford, nudges fellow U.S. senator John McCafferty, trying to wake him up for a quorum call. McCafferty jolts up and absentmindedly blares out, "Opposed Sir. Diametrically opposed." He repeats the startled-from-dozing outburst toward the end of the movie, thus totaling the only two scenes the actor ever played in a Hollywood movie. This insignificant appearance with minimal speaking is ironic, because in real life, the actor playing the doddering McCafferty was actually a politician and a loquacious man whose contributions were anything but insignificant. His name was Henry Fountain Ashurst, and his roots in northern Arizona run deep.

In 1874, a rancher named William Henry Ashurst and his pregnant wife, Sarah, were moving their sheep from California to Arizona, which was a multi-year process. On September 13, 1874, Mrs. Ashurst gave birth to a son in the back of an uncovered wagon in Winnemucca, Nevada. The proud parents named the boy Henry Fountain Ashurst, the middle name after an Uncle Fountain.

The following year, the family arrived in Arizona and soon settled on a ranch nine miles south of present-day Williams. Because of a drought in 1877, they again had to look for a new place to live. At Anderson Mesa, a dozen miles southeast of Flagstaff, the family found a box canyon with a spring running through it about a mile east of present-day Ashurst Lake. William moved his family, which eventually included ten children, to this location and built a ranch.

Henry Fountain Ashurst. *Library of Congress Prints and Photographs Division, George Grantham Bain Collection.*

It was in the cabin that young Henry, à la Abraham Lincoln, learned to read and write. Life on the frontier ranch was rustic with few amenities. Butter was kept cold by storing it in crocks submerged in the spring. Allegedly, and in keeping with typical western lore, William was said to have buried five-

and ten-pound cans filled with gold coins on his property, and supposedly, the gold has never been found.

After the arrival of the railroad in Flagstaff in 1882, local leaders realized the community needed a school and opened one the following year. It was a classic one-room schoolhouse with a sole teacher for all grades, Eva Marshall. William moved the family into Flagstaff so his children could attend, but the Ashursts continued to use the ranch on a seasonal basis until 1890. After William died in the Grand Canyon in 1901, the family sold the ranch to the Babbitt brothers. Today, the Ashurst Cabin is preserved at the Pioneer Living History Museum north of Phoenix.

Henry Fountain Ashurst began working at the age of twelve on the family's ranch, and he spent years as a range rider and lumberyard laborer. In his later years, he remembered that his interest in politics was aroused in 1893 by saloon keeper and county sheriff Sandy Donahue, whom Henry worked under as a jailer. This may have been the start of his serious contemplation about politics, but he had thought about it earlier, albeit perhaps as the wandering daydreams of a child. About a decade earlier, when he was only ten years old, he scripted in one of his school notebooks, "Henry Fountain Ashurst, United States Senator."[1]

As a teenager, Ashurst became fascinated with public speaking and attended as many speeches as he possibly could. He honed his own skills and became a master orator. He once explained this passion by saying, "I simply love speaking—just as one may like maple syrup, Beethoven, Verdi, or Longfellow, Kipling, or Shakespeare—one hardly knows why."[2] This early passion for politics and public speaking kick-started Henry's lifelong career as a politician. He said, "I could throw fifty-six-pound words clear across the Grand Canyon. As a matter of course, I went into politics."[3]

In between stints as a lawyer in Williams and Prescott, Ashurst served in both the House and Senate of the Territorial Legislature, where, in 1899, he introduced the bill that officially established the Northern Arizona Normal School. From 1905 to 1908, he was Coconino County district attorney, and when Arizona became a state in 1912, he and Marcus Smith were chosen as its first senators.

Ashurst would stay in office for twenty-nine years until 1941. He became famous for his flowery language. Once, when asked about his well-documented tendency to change viewpoints on certain topics, Ashurst said:

Whoever in his public services is handcuffed and shackled by the vice of consistency will be a man not free to act as various questions come before

Home of Henry and Elizabeth Ashurst at the southeast corner of Park Street and Aspen Avenue when it also housed Flagstaff's first weather station. *Kevin Schindler's collection.*

> *him from time to time; he will be a statesman locked in a prison house, keys to which are in the keeping of days and events that are dead. Let me quote Emerson: "A foolish consistency is the hobgoblin of little minds, adored by little statesmen."*[4]

Ashurst openly celebrated his way with words. He once puffed:

> *I suffer from cacoethes loquendi, a mania or itch for talking, and from vanity…and morbidity, and, as is obvious to everyone who knows me, an inborn, an inveterate flair for histrionics…I am pachydermatous…I am a veritable peripatetic bifurcated volcano on behalf of Democratic principles.*[5]

In 1904, Henry married Elizabeth McEvoy Renoe. She was the observer at Flagstaff's first weather station, which was located in the couple's house, which is still standing at the southeast corner of Park Street and Aspen Avenue. Elizabeth died in 1939 while Henry was still in office. He continued living in Washington, D.C., for another two decades before his death on May 31, 1962—just a week before the release of *Advise and Consent.* He and Elizabeth are buried at Sacred Heart Cemetery in Prescott.

From his humble beginnings in Flagstaff, Henry Fountain Ashurst remains one of Arizona's most distinguished and influential citizens. His memory is preserved in the names of several local landmarks, including Northern Arizona University's Ashurst Hall and Ashurst Lake near Anderson Mesa.

COCONINO COUNTY

One day in 1889, a train pulled into Flagstaff and briefly stopped. As passengers stepped off to stretch their legs, they were shocked by the gruesome sight of someone firing shots into a hanging body that had been set aflame. They didn't stick around long enough to find out the truth of what was happening. They all scampered back on board the train and were probably quite relieved when it pulled out of the station. The display was, in fact, not as morbid as it seemed, but it nevertheless captured the anger of locals suffering through the latest episode in the ongoing saga of trying to create a new county.

Arizona was first declared a territory and claimed by Jefferson Davis, president of the so-called Confederate States of America, in the early 1860s. President of the United States, Abraham Lincoln, trumped the Confederate Arizona Territory and created the Arizona Territory in 1863 on the alignment it has today. In 1864, it was broken up into four counties—Yavapai, Pima, Yuma and Mohave. Yavapai County, which was about the size of the entire state of New York, encompassed much of northern Arizona, including the future site of Flagstaff. After the railroad arrived in 1882 and the community began to grow, residents who had to go to the county seat of Prescott found the trip to be very long and inconvenient. They soon began calling for the division of Yavapai County into smaller units, and one of them featured Flagstaff as the county seat. Supporters held many meetings, and regional newspapers—particularly in Flagstaff and Prescott—weighed in and often sparred about the advantages and disadvantages of the plan.

In 1887, at the Fourteenth Territorial Legislative Assembly, William Henry Ashurst, the father of future senator Henry Fountain Ashurst, served as an assemblyman representing Flagstaff. He promoted a bill calling for the creation of Frisco County, which was named after the San Francisco Peaks. The bill was narrowly defeated, but Ashurst succeeded in building awareness about the need for the new county.

Flagstaff boosters continued their efforts with one major change: to be consistent with the names of other Arizona counties, many of which were named after Native American groups, a lumberman, Denis (Matt) Riordan, proposed the name *Coconino* after the Hopi name for the Havasupai Indians of the Grand Canyon, *Cohonino*. At the Fifteenth Legislative Assembly in 1889, assemblymen passed a new county bill, but to the dismay and outrage of many, Territorial Governor Lewis Wolfley vetoed the measure. This is what spurred the scene the train passengers had witnessed. Local residents were so upset with Wolfley that they hung an effigy of him, lit it on fire and shot it full of holes. Whether or not the passengers ever found out the unfortunate figure wasn't a real person is unknown. In any case, it made for a memorable event for all involved.

More debate and discussion about the creation of a new county followed over the next two years. In 1891, a committee that included Riordan and William Munds, a namesake of several local features, formed and drafted a bill titled, "An Act to Create the County of Coconino." Under this measure, the new county would encompass a little more than two thirds of the area of Yavapai County and assume one third of Yavapai's debt. The county would include Flagstaff, the Grand Canyon and parts of the Navajo and Hopi nations.

During their meeting in 1891, the members of the Sixteenth Legislative Assembly passed the bill. This time, there would be no veto and no effigies burned, because new Territorial Governor John Irwin signed the bill into law on February 19, 1891.

Perhaps the most recognizable symbol of Coconino County is its beautiful stone courthouse at the northeast corner of Birch Avenue and San Francisco Street. It was built several years after the county was established. Before its doors were opened, temporary

Denis "Matt" Riordan. *Kevin Schindler's collection.*

Coconino County Courthouse. *Kevin Schindler's collection.*

offices were needed, so for $1,000 per year, the country rented space on the second floor of the Babbitt Brothers Building, which was located at the northwest corner of Aspen Avenue and San Francisco Street. In May 1894, local residents who were attending a special town meeting formally approved a bond issue for constructing a new courthouse. Federal law required that Congress approve all such territory bonds, so Riordan was chosen to take it to Washington, D.C., to get the approval. Construction of the new courthouse began in October 1894 and was finished the following year. The primary building material was "Coconino Red," a locally-sourced sandstone of the Moenkopi Formation (more about that later). Actually, the courthouse was not quite finished until years later. The southwest corner of the building featured a four-sided tower that stood above the rest of the two-story building. Each side was supposed to include a clock, but a lack of funding kept this from happening until the courthouse was expanded in 1925.

Modern-day Coconino County remains expansive. By area, it's larger than nine states, including New Jersey, Massachusetts and Vermont, and is the second-largest county in the United States behind only San Bernardino County in California. While it maintains much of the charm of yesteryear, one thing residents can no longer expect to see is a burning body strung up next to the railroad tracks.

ARIZONA RED

*M*uch of Flagstaff's identity is tied to its characteristic buildings, which were constructed from a variety of local materials. These stones include the fossil-rich Kaibab Limestone and a volcanic rock known locally as malpais basalt, which is often pitted and masked with green lichen. Another popular building stone that was used for years in Flagstaff is the rich, red sandstone nicknamed "Arizona Red."

From a geological perspective, Arizona Red is part of the Moenkopi Formation and is exposed in western states including California, Nevada, Arizona, Utah, Colorado and New Mexico. Its layers of sandstone, siltstone and mudstone preserve the record of an extensive coastal plain where sand and mud periodically settled out of the water some 240 million years ago. Moenkopi rocks typically extend in thin layers that often feature ripple marks and animal trackways that are frozen in time. The rock is found throughout much of northern Arizona, and its history as a building material dates back more than a millennium, when the Sinagua would use it to construct their buildings at what is now known as the Wupatki National Monument.

Early Flagstaff builders typically used wood for their structures, and since Ponderosa pine trees covered much of the Flagstaff area, wood was inexpensive and easy to access. However, wood has one significant problem—it's highly flammable. Several fires in the mid-1880s razed blocks of wooden buildings located at the original town site of Flagstaff, which is a mile west of today's downtown. In the past, builders had occasionally used stone for building foundations, but after the fires, they realized locally produced brick or rock was more practical as a primary building material.

Businessman Patrick B. Brannen used Arizona Red to build a structure across from the railroad depot, about one mile east of the original town site. This helped form the basis of the new downtown area that remains today. Other builders soon followed suit, and Arizona Red became extremely popular, not only for its resistance to fire, but also for its rich red color and apparent durability. It was used in the construction of many classic structures, including the McMillan Building (built in the mid- to late 1880s), Santa Fe Railway depot (1889), the Coconino County Jail (1891), Old Main at Northern Arizona University (mid-to-late 1890s), the Weatherford Hotel (late 1890s) and the Federated Community Church (1906). The rock was also used to build many structures outside Flagstaff, including the Los Angeles County Courthouse (1889).

Most of the rock was mined from a fifty-foot-thick, seven-hundred-foot-wide deposit lying a mile east of downtown Flagstaff. It was here, along the southern edge of McMillan Mesa and just north of the intersection of today's Route 66 and Ponderosa Parkway, that Charles Begg organized

Old Main on the campus of Northern Arizona University. *Kevin Schindler's collection.*

Arizona Sandstone Company operation. *Kevin Schindler's collection.*

a mining operation in the mid-1880s. He sold it, along with the 160-acre parcel surrounding the deposit, in 1887 to businessman L.H. Padgham. This native Californian retained Begg, who served as general manager and developed many contracts with businesses looking to purchase the rock. The fortunes of the operation changed dramatically with an order for five hundred boxcars of stone to be used for the Los Angeles courthouse project. Padgham brought on several partners and incorporated as the Arizona Sandstone Company the following year. At the height of operation, eighty workers used saws, drills, explosives and a network of ropes and pulleys to harvest and move the rock. A railroad spur ran to the quarry, and workers loaded the material directly into boxcars and sent them off. Many of the laborers, often with their families, lived in boardinghouses and other facilities at the site.

Business was brisk for several years, but like mining in other parts of the state, it proved to be a boom-and-bust venture. Production peaked from the time of incorporation to about 1892, when a half-dozen train cars of rock were sent from the quarry daily. By then, it had become the second-greatest source of revenue in Flagstaff, behind only the lumber mills, but the bottom was about to fall out of the market. With the devastating Panic of 1893, which among other things collapsed construction across the United States, the Arizona Red enterprise took a steep downturn.

Future builders, particularly Northern Arizona University, continued to occasionally use Arizona Red, but its heyday lasted only a few years. Alternate building materials and the discovery that Arizona Red weathers horribly in other regions ensured the eventual demise of this rock as a primary building material. The last rock came out of the quarry in the 1970s for use in fixing a building in Chicago.

While the Arizona Red mining operation is long in the past, several beautiful buildings in Flagstaff, as well as a large gap in the rocks a mile east of town, serve as reminders of the once-thriving mining industry here.

THE 1894 LOWELL EXPEDITION

Since the late 1890s, a white, birthday cake–shaped building has been perched atop a mesa just a mile west of downtown Flagstaff. This landmark serves as a constant reminder of the community's scientific heritage, and in particular, the contributions of a man who journeyed to the wilds of Arizona on a quest to find life on Mars.

The story starts in Massachusetts with Percival Lowell, the son of a wealthy Boston family whose members included businessmen, educators, judges, writers, industrialists, ministers, philanthropists and architects. Born in 1855, Lowell grew up in Boston and attended Harvard University, majoring in mathematics. At the age of thirty-nine, after an eight-year stint managing the finances of his family's textile business followed by a decade of living overseas, Lowell became fascinated with the possibility of life on Mars and planned to build his own astronomical research facility to carry out studies.

Lowell decided to launch an expedition to Arizona Territory in order to find an ideal location for the new observatory. He wanted to choose a place that was removed from eastern U.S. cities, where factory smoke and the glare from electric lights blotted out stars and planets. A dry climate and high elevation were also ideal, and all of these characteristics can be found in the American Southwest. Lowell would later write:

> *Astronomy now demands bodily abstraction of its devotee.... To see into the beyond requires purity; in the medium now as formerly in the man. As little air as may be and that only of the best is obligatory to its enterprise,*

and the securing it makes him perforce a hermit from his own kind. He must abandon cities and forego plains. Only in places raised above and aloof from his fellow man can he profitably pursue his search.[6]

Lowell himself would not join the expedition. Instead, he hired a young astronomer named Andrew Douglass to carry out the work. Traveling alone, Douglass was to visit various sites in Arizona and carry with him a six-inch telescope that Lowell had taken to the Orient in 1892. Douglass was also given instruments to gauge atmospheric conditions. Based on these observations, Lowell would choose the ideal site for his observatory.

Douglass left Massachusetts on February 18, 1894, on a train that transported him from the conveniences and luxuries of the civilized East to the rough-and-tumble Arizona frontier where stagecoach drivers still carried rifles to ward off such notorious outlaws as the legendary Apache Kid. Douglass arrived in Benson, Arizona, on March 7 and took a stagecoach down to Tombstone, a mining town that was just a dozen years removed from the infamous gunfight at the O.K. Corral. Over a five-day period, Douglass set up the telescope at three different locations in the area. He viewed stars such as Capella, Sirius and Aldebaran to evaluate each location's "seeing," or the inherent quality of celestial viewing based on local atmospheric conditions. He also recorded temperature, atmospheric pressure, wind and evaporation rates, which he would compare to other locations around the territory.

Douglass then packed the equipment on a stagecoach and headed back to Benson, where he caught a train northwest to Tucson. From March 11 to 16, he tested three sites in Tuscon, including Sentinel Peak, which is commonly known as "A" Mountain today and is where University of Arizona students regularly paint a large letter "A" that is visible from miles around. Douglass also stopped at the University of Arizona to visit with a faculty member. Little did Douglass know that he would live the last half-century of his life in Tucson, where he made his most famous scientific contributions while working at the university. He not only founded the Steward Observatory, but he also established the science of dendrochronology (tree ring dating).

From Tucson, Douglass took a train northwest to Tempe and from March 17 to 27, he tested two stations. One was at Tempe Butte, which is known today as Tempe's version of "A" Mountain, where Arizona State University students paint their own large "A," albeit in different colors than those of their rivals in Tucson. The butte is also the current site of Arizona State University's football stadium.

After Tempe, Douglass took a stagecoach northwest over the extremely rough Black Canyon Highway to Prescott, where from March 28 to April 3, he tested more sites. On April 3, he again loaded his equipment onto a train and traveled north to Ash Fork.

Later that day, Douglass took another train east to the lumber town of Flagstaff and arrived just after dark. He checked into a room at the Arizona Central Bank and Hotel and later conducted a few seeing tests. The next day, Douglass set up the telescope on a mesa just above the Arizona Lumber and Timber Company, the largest lumber mill in town. This was the eleventh site Douglass had tested on the expedition, and while he would visit three more locations in the Flagstaff area, site eleven is where Percival Lowell would ultimately build his observatory.

Appropriately, Flagstaff was then nicknamed the Skylight City because of the brilliance of stars visible from its environs. While that name eventually faded, the darkness and overall excellence of Flagstaff's skies for astronomical viewing remained. In 1958, Flagstaff leaders created the world's first lighting ordinance, and in 2001, the community was designated the first International Dark Sky City in recognition of this cherished natural resource and the lighting codes the community has enacted to safeguard these conditions.

Site eleven, on the mesa later nicknamed Mars Hill. The six-inch telescope Andrew Douglass used for celestial viewing is covered by a white tarp while an unidentified man sits atop a horse. *Lowell Observatory Archives.*

Like in other communities Douglass had visited, Flagstaff's leaders saw the benefit of having an observatory in their area. They thought it could provide jobs and, more importantly, bring prestige to an area that was still building its identity. On the day Douglass established site eleven, Denis (Matt) Riordan, one of three brothers who owned the mill, paid him a visit. Douglass, ever the thorough scientist, had tested three other locations in the Flagstaff area by April 11: Elden "Mesa," Wing Mountain and a hill near A1 Ranch known as A-1 Mountain.

Percival Lowell, anxious for his observatory to be built so he could begin viewing Mars, sent a telegram to Douglass on April 16 telling of his decision to locate the new facility in Flagstaff. A few days later, Douglass received a letter signed by eighty-two Flagstaff citizens pledging their support for the new observatory. The letter stated that the community would build a road up the side of the mesa to the new facility and deeded the necessary land he needed to build the observatory.

On April 21, 1894, four days after the pledge letter had been signed, Lowell telegrammed Douglass his decision to build the observatory at site eleven. As for the precise location, Douglass chose a knoll about a half mile to the north where the gentler slope allowed for easier construction of a road to the top of the mesa. The site was about one mile from downtown Flagstaff and easily visible from town. On April 23, Douglass and some helpers broke ground on the facility, which would feature borrowed telescopes and a dome to house them. Lowell arrived on May 28, and with little fanfare, officially opened his astronomical research facility and began his search for life on Mars. He soon replaced the borrowed equipment with his own twenty-four-inch-diameter, thirty-two-foot-long telescope and the birthday cake–shaped dome to house it. More buildings would be added through the years, but this telescope and dome still stand on the edge of the mesa as a beacon of knowledge and learning.

When looking back at the expedition, Lowell clearly deemed the atmospheric conditions in Flagstaff sufficient for building the observatory here. However, a combination of other factors ensured Flagstaff was the ideal site. Extraordinary community support and politicking by residents like Riordan certainly helped. Perhaps an even greater factor was the timing of the project. Percival Lowell wanted the observatory to be established as quickly as possible. By the time Douglass arrived in Flagstaff, he had been site testing for a month—longer than Lowell originally anticipated. The atmospheric conditions in Flagstaff were good, community support was strong and transportation was adequate, so Lowell, anxious to have

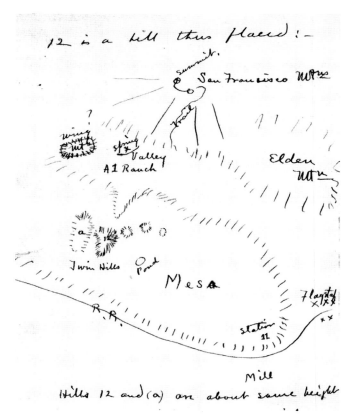

Left: Drawing by Andrew Douglass showing the locations of the testing sites in Flagstaff. *Lowell Observatory Archives.*

Below: Telegram from Percival Lowell to Andrew Douglass indicating his decision to establish his observatory in Flagstaff. *Lowell Observatory Archives.*

telescopes ready for an upcoming, favorable appearance of Mars, chose Flagstaff. Had Douglass been in any of the other locations where conditions were favorable, such as Tombstone, the observatory could quite possibly have been built there. In any event, Flagstaff was the chosen location and Lowell Observatory became the first permanent scientific institution in Flagstaff. It helped establish the community as a center for scientific research and laid the groundwork for the development of other research facilities in the area, such as the Museum of Northern Arizona (1928), the U.S. Naval Observatory's Flagstaff Station (1955) and the U.S. Geological Survey's Astrogeology Branch (1963). And it all started with a one-man expedition through the untamed lands of the Arizona Territory.

A Well-Traveled Rock

More than a century ago, the leader of a prominent family in northern Arizona stole a rock from a mining engineer and hauled it to his store at the Grand Canyon so his patrons could ogle it. Or so the yarn has been laughingly spun by the grandchildren of John Verkamp and Daniel Moreau Barringer. Such anecdotes notwithstanding, the rock in question has quite a story—one that begins in outer space and ends in Flagstaff. It serves as a great example of northern Arizona's historic ties to its natural landscape.

The tale begins around fifty thousand years ago when a meteorite about the size of a commercial airliner screamed through Earth's atmosphere at some eight to twelve miles per second and slammed into the limestone bedrock thirty-five miles east of present-day Flagstaff. The impact resulted in a chasm three-quarters of a mile across and 570 feet deep that people today call Coon Mountain, Barringer Crater, Canyon Diablo Crater and Meteor Crater. Remains of the meteorite, which are rich in nickel and iron and range in size from microscopic particles to boulder-sized fragments, littered the nearby landscape.

Late nineteenth and early twentieth century scientists debated the crater's origins. Many believed it was the result of a volcanic steam eruption while others recognized its true extraterrestrial origins. One supporter of this extraterrestrial "impact" theory was mining engineer and businessman Daniel Moreau Barringer. He was intrigued by the bits of nickel-iron rock and believed the main body of the impactor must still exist, buried

Aerial view of Meteor Crater. *Michael Collier.*

underneath the crater, and is waiting for some enterprising person to uncover it. Barringer thought he was the man for the job and envisioned mining the nickel-iron lode, which he estimated would be worth around $1 billion. Perhaps this apparition of riches is what inspired Barringer's name for the company he founded in 1903 to carry out the work. He called it the Standard Iron Company, an evocative take on billionaire John D. Rockefeller's oil refining business's name, the Standard Oil Company.

While Barringer pursued these anticipated mining riches, another entrepreneur in the area was laying his own path to prosperity. His name was John George Verkamp, and his sisters, Emma, Mary and Matilda, had married the Babbitt brothers, David, Charles and Edward, respectively. In 1889 Verkamp had set up a tent at the South Rim of the Grand Canyon and sold souvenirs to tourists. In 1906 he built a permanent store just east of the recently completed Hopi House, which itself was one hundred yards or so east of the El Tovar Hotel. Soon after opening, Verkamp somehow acquired a 535-pound fragment of the Meteor Crater impactor and put it on public display outside of his shop. For most of the following eighty years, the meteorite fragment sat there, though it did disappear on a couple of occasions. Once, Verkamp's son, Jack, and grandson, Mike, arrived at the shop and found that the meteorite had been moved to block the front door as a prank by a group of people who were never identified. The Verkamps had the last laugh though, because they found blood on the entry where one of the pranksters apparently paid for the joke. Another time, the Verkamps went outside to find that the meteorite was missing. They eventually found it a few miles away and figured it must have been another prank that had perhaps been perpetrated by some local urchins or friends of the Verkamps.

In 1988 Mike Verkamp, who was then operating the shop, remodeled the facility in an effort to restore the original character of the building and its contents. Among other things, he installed a new oak floor and moved the meteorite inside. He hired a handyman named Don Kelsey to design and build an artistic stand that could handle the immense weight of the rock. Kelsey fashioned a metal pedestal whose base went through the floor and anchored into the bedrock beneath the basement. The meteorite was displayed on that stand for the next twenty years.

In 2008, the Verkamp family decided to close the shop after 102 years in operation. The decision marked the passing of an era, as this was the last family-owned business in the National Park Service. The family had to consider what would happen to the two historic and popular display

The Verkamp Meteorite on display at Lowell Observatory. *Kevin Schindler's collection.*

pieces inside the shop, a classic Louis Akin painting, *Evening–Grand Canyon*, and the meteorite. The family arranged for the painting to stay in the shop, but they wanted to find a new home for the meteorite; ideally, it would go to a place that would appreciate its heritage. Siblings Steve, a former U.S. magistrate judge in Flagstaff, and Susie Verkamp, as representatives of all of the grandchildren of John Verkamp, contacted Drew Barringer, grandson of Daniel Moreau Barringer. Barringer was the president of the Barringer Crater Company, the modern-day owners of the crater, and he also served on the advisory board of Lowell Observatory. Barringer told the Verkamps that the Meteor Crater visitor center already had quite a large collection of meteorite material, but that perhaps Lowell Observatory would be interested in displaying it. This seemed like an ideal location, since Lowell was in the business of studying objects from space. Observatory staff members were quite receptive of the opportunity to display this scientific, cultural and historic relic.

In October 2008, Steve Verkamp joined National Park Service personnel and two Lowell representatives—Director of Technical Services Ralph Nye and Outreach Manager Kevin Schindler—in removing the meteorite from the Verkamp shop. The rock was lifted with a boom crane and rolled onto a Lowell pick-up truck. To remove the stand, the group went into the basement, where Nye and Verkamp took turns with a hacksaw and cut away the base of the stand until it broke free. They then went back upstairs, lifted the stand out of the floor and loaded it onto the truck.

Back at Lowell, workers mounted the rock onto its stand in the lobby of the Steele Visitor Center. On June 6, 2009, Lowell Observatory hosted an unveiling ceremony for the meteorite and accompanying display. Dozens of people gathered to celebrate the heritage of the "Verkamp Meteorite," including John Verkamp's grandchildren Steve, Susie and former state senator, John. Daniel Moreau Barringer's grandson, Drew Barringer; Lowell Observatory founder, Percival Lowell's grandnephew, Bill Putnam; and Carolyn Shoemaker, widow of geologist Gene Shoemaker, who, in the 1960s, proved with certainty the extraterrestrial origins of Meteor Crater, were also in attendance. It was a fitting tribute to this well-traveled rock and to the inspiration for the pursuit of knowledge that it has given millions of people for well over a century.

A GIANT POCKMARK ON THE EARTH

One of the many enjoyable things about reading books is the unexpected discovery of some obscure fact or story that connects people and places. Such is the case with a book published back in 1953 that was a sort of travelogue recalling a family trip across the United States. The author, who is known more for his flying escapades than his books, wrote about passing through northern Arizona:

> *There's a great, steep hollow in the mist...hard, reddish-yellow walls, broken, crumbling slopes, cupping a mile-wide crater. See the deep, blue sky above, through which a meteor once hurtled to make this giant pockmark on the earth. My mother, my Uncle Charles, and I stand on the blasted rim, near Winslow, Arizona. A hot wind blows dust against our eyes, and whistles through stone crevices. Almost a thousand feet below us lies the brush-spotted desert floor, a group of abandoned mine buildings in its center. Far in the distance, a puff of dust marks another car's struggle with the sands. Beyond that, there's not a sign of life for as far as we can see.*

> *It's late summer of 1916. I'm driving our Saxon car from Little Falls (Minnesota) to California. We've been over thirty days on the road, and we've been pushing fairly hard. Weather and mechanical troubles have held [us] up—a worn-out timer-trigger in Iowa, mud in Mississippi (oh, those dismal hotel rooms, where we waited for the roads to dry!), a broken spring-bolt in Kansas, a wheel shimmy that started on the Raton Pass. The list*

is long; we add a few items almost every day, and we still have half a thousand miles to go. My uncle picks up a chunk of brownish rock. I wish we could find a fragment of the meteor.[7]

While brief, the account is interesting for several reasons. First, it offers us a glimpse into a significant time in the history of American tourism and travel. Henry Ford had pioneered the process of mass-producing automobiles in 1913 with his introduction of moving assembly lines. Soon, families could afford to buy their own cars and were eager to use them to travel across the country. This led to the development of a better and more extensive road system that included a transcontinental highway called the National Old Trails Road. In the West, this route often followed historic trails such as the Beale Wagon Road, and it would later serve as the basis for part of Route 66, and eventually, Interstate 40. The National Old Trails Road passed through northern Arizona in 1915. Our author and his family, traveling just a year later, likely took advantage of this new roadway on their journey west.

The second noteworthy aspect of the account is that it recalls an early visit by tourists to Meteor Crater. At the time, Daniel Moreau Barringer was still mining the crater in the hopes of discovering the very large, and in his mind, very valuable mass of nickel that had created the crater. We know today that Barringer was searching for a ghost, since modern science shows that the majority of the impactor had vaporized. However, Meteor Crater still proved valuable, not for its mineral riches, but for its combination of scientific significance as the best-preserved impact crater known on Earth and an ideal analogy to similar features on the Moon and its significance as a destination spot for tourists. This duality is common at other sites around northern Arizona, including the Grand Canyon, Sunset Crater, the San Francisco Peaks, the Museum of Northern Arizona and Lowell Observatory.

The third, and perhaps most breathtaking, feature of the story involves the identity of the author and circumstances relating to his recollection of the Meteor Crater visit. The book, titled *The Spirit of St. Louis*, is Charles Lindbergh's autobiographical account of his 1927 solo flight from New York to Paris. Throughout the narrative, Lindbergh injects memories from his life that came to mind as he struggled to stay awake during his thirty-three-and-a-half-hour-long journey.

Seventeen hours into the flight, and thirty-eight hours since he had last slept, Lindbergh was dead reckoning his way over the Atlantic when he

Charles Lindbergh. *Kevin Schindler's collection.*

dreamily thought of that long-ago visit to northern Arizona as a fourteen-year-old. And that is how a memory of Meteor Crater become a footnote in the story of one of the most celebrated and remarkable events of modern times.

Lindbergh's Meteor Crater story doesn't end there. In the summer of 1929, two years after his transoceanic adventure, Lindbergh flew over

Grove Karl Gilbert's wide-angle photograph of Meteor Crater from 1891. *United States Geological Survey.*

northern Arizona while helping to develop the infrastructure needed for the first commercial transcontinental flights. During that expedition, he took the first aerial photograph of Meteor Crater, and he also chose Winslow as the site for one of the twelve refueling stops for the transcontinental service. The Winslow-Lindbergh Regional Airport is still in service today.

Lindbergh also stopped several times at Flagstaff's first airport, Koch (pronounced like "Coke") Field. This airport was located in the Doney Park area northeast of town and was named after the general manager of the Arizona Lumber and Timber Company and one-time Flagstaff mayor, Ignacio "Tony" Koch. The field opened in 1928 and operated for two decades before being replaced by the larger Pulliam Airport located three miles south of Flagstaff.

CLYDE TOMBAUGH DISCOVERS PLUTO

On January 14, 1929, a twenty-three-year old farmer from Burdett, Kansas, stepped onto a train for a ride that took him from the cornfields of the Midwest to telescopes in the Southwest, and ultimately, into the history books. His father imparted some advice, "Clyde, make yourself useful and beware of easy women."[8] His full name was Clyde William Tombaugh, and within a year, he would go from helping his family harvest crops to discovering a new planet at Lowell Observatory.

Tombaugh officially began working at Lowell Observatory on January 15, 1929. To earn his monthly salary of $125, plus living quarters on the second story of the observatory's administration building that is known today as the Slipher Building, Tombaugh shoveled coal and wood into the administration building's furnace, cleared snow off telescope domes and presented the daily afternoon tour to visitors. Tombaugh also led the observatory's search for a theoretical ninth planet; on clear, moonless nights, he made photographic plates of selected areas of the night sky. These plates recorded an area of the sky that was about the size of a fist held at arm's length, and with a one-hour exposure, they captured an average of about three hundred thousand star images. During the day, Tombaugh examined pairs of these plates that contained images of the same portion of the sky but that were taken a few days apart. His job was to use a device called a blink comparator to look at every image from one plate to the other and see if any of the stars changed position. Most of them did not, but those that did represented a possible planet that moved relative to the background stars. Later in life, Tombaugh

Clyde Tombaugh at the thirteen-inch telescope he used to discover Pluto. *Lowell Observatory Archives.*

estimated he spent seven thousand hours at the blink comparator eyepiece during his fourteen-year career at Lowell Observatory, which comes out to an average of five hundred hours per year or sixty-three full working days.

Tuesday, February 18, 1930, started out as a typical day for Tombaugh. He woke up at about 7:00 a.m. and drove down Mars Hill to downtown

Flagstaff. He picked up the observatory's mail at the post office, which was then located in the Nackard Building on North San Francisco Street (Arizona Handmade Gallery and Aspen Sports occupy this building as of 2019). Then, Tombaugh headed to breakfast at his favorite restaurant—he ate most of his meals here, in fact—the Black Cat Café, whose building was later home to the Hong Kong Cafe and Karma Sushi Bar & Grill. After breakfast, Tombaugh returned to the observatory, and by 9:00 a.m., he was in the blink comparator room and settling in for another tedious day of staring through the comparator's microscope eyepiece. The plates he examined that day captured a portion of the constellation Gemini. He spent three hours at the comparator that morning, occasionally taking breaks from the mentally rigorous work and blinking to keep his eyes from blurring images together and his concentration from faltering.

At noon, Tombaugh drove to the café for lunch and returned by 1:00 p.m. for another marathon blinking session. At about 4:00 p.m., he noticed a faint image popping in and out of view. He had been doing these tests long enough to know when he had an obvious planet suspect, and this definitely was one. With mounting excitement, he spent the next forty-five minutes making measurements and checking a backup set of plates taken with a five-inch telescope mounted to the main thirteen-inch instrument. Sure enough, the images also appeared on these plates in the exact expected position.

Tombaugh called in astronomer Carl Lampland from across the hall and then hurried to Director V.M. Slipher's office. With as much composure as he could muster, Tombaugh announced, "I have found your Planet X." The three rushed back to the blink comparator room and confirmed the planetary nature of the object. For additional confirmation, Slipher instructed Tombaugh to re-photograph the sky that night. It would be one of the most excruciating nights of young Tombaugh's life. At about 6:00 p.m., he drove to town and repeated his usual trip of picking up mail and eating at the café. After his meal, he dashed outside and was aghast to see clouds covering the sky. How do you pass time and keep your sanity knowing that you are close to becoming only the third person to ever discover a planet? First, he went to the Orpheum Theatre and watched Gary Cooper star in the film *The Virginian*, which is based on a book by Owen Wister. After leaving the theater, Tombaugh saw that the sky was still clouded over, and exasperated, he drove back to the observatory, sorted mail and tried to read. Hoping to will the clouds away, he loaded photographic plates into their holders in anticipation of some clearing, but alas, the clouds refused to move. By 2:00 a.m., the Gemini area of the sky was too far west, so Tombaugh called it a night. Of all the days he would live in his ninety plus years, none would ever be like this one.

For the next three weeks, Tombaugh and his colleagues at Lowell quietly studied the new world through telescopes, took a slew of photographs and evaluated relevant astronomical data. Staff members had agreed to keep the news secret until they could confirm the planetary nature of the body. By mid-March, the team had gathered enough evidence to justify the announcement of this object as a new planet. The question then became, "When should we announce this discovery?" Observatory staff chose March 13, because that would have been Percival Lowell's seventy-fifth birthday. It was a fitting tribute to the man whose inspiration led to the discovery of this new planet. Furthermore, William Herschel discovered the planet Uranus on March 13, 1781.

On the evening of March 12, V.M. Slipher sent a telegram to the Harvard College Observatory. From this, officials created *Harvard College Observatory Announcement Card 108*, which officially announced the new planet's discovery and was circulated the following day. Slipher wrote a more detailed account of the discovery and printed it as a *Lowell Observatory Observation Circular*, which was also released on March 13. Astronomer Carl Lampland was busy as well presenting the Lowell Prize to the top mathematics student at Arizona State Teacher's College at Flagstaff on behalf of Lowell Observatory. The ceremony took place in front of an audience of five hundred at Ashurst Hall. As part of his speech, Lampland made the first public announcement of the new planet's discovery. Few, if any, of the audience members heard this important message, since the soft-spoken Lampland could not be heard in the uncarpeted, echo-filled room.

Once the story hit the newswires, observatory staff spent most of their time handling a glut of calls, telegrams and visits from the media, astronomers and other interested parties. Newspaper headlines from around the world lauded the discovery, and the name Flagstaff was soon famous. In Burdett, Kansas, Clyde's father, Muron, received a call from the editor of the *Tiller and Toiler*, the county's weekly newspaper, asking him about the discovery. Mr. Tombaugh was stunned, not having heard the news until now. His twenty-four-year-old son had promised not to tell anyone about the discovery, so he hadn't, not even his parents!

Buzz of the discovery soon focused on what to call this new member of the solar system. People from around the world sent letters and telegrams to Lowell with their suggestions. W.E.D. Stokes Jr., son of a New York

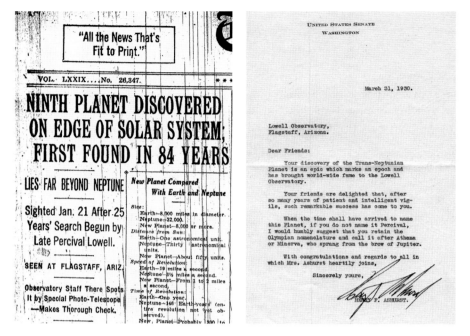

Left: Front page of the *New York Times*, March 14, 1930. *Lowell Observatory Archives.*

Right: March 31, 1930 letter from Henry Fountain Ashurst to Lowell Observatory offering his congratulations on Pluto's discovery. *Lowell Observatory Archives.*

property developer and millionaire, wrote, "Suggest you name new planet after last word in [the] dictionary, which is zymal, the last word in planets." A man from New Hampshire wrote, "If I had discovered the new trans-Neptunian planet, I would name it 'Jean' after my two-year baby girl. I do not know the definition of the name Jean, but it means 'everything' to me. This letter is not a crank."[9]

The matter was finally settled in May, with a *Lowell Observatory Observation Circular* written by Slipher, dated May 1. The beginning of this paper discusses the new planet's orbit and then turns to naming.

> *It seems time now that this body should be given a name of its own. Many names have been suggested and among them Minerva and Pluto have been very popular. But, as Minerva has long been used for one of the asteroids it is really not available for this object. However, Pluto seems very appropriate and we are proposing to the American Astronomical Society and to the Royal Astronomical Society, that this name be given*

it. As far as we know Pluto was first suggested by Miss Venetia Burney, aged 11, of Oxford, England.

Slipher also suggested a scientific symbol for Pluto—a combination of its first two letters, P and L. These were Percival Lowell's initials and served as another tribute to the late founder of the observatory. By the end of the month, the name Pluto had extended from scientific circles to the public; a headline in the May 30, 1930 edition of the *Coconino Sun* reads, "New Planet Gets Name of Pluto." The new body now had a name, one that has since been inextricably tied to Flagstaff.

A Grand Bicycle Race

*F*lagstaff is a bicycle-friendly community with designated bike lanes running along many of the major roads in town. It also has a citywide network of nonmotorized, shared-use pathways that make up the Flagstaff Urban Trail System (FUTS) and bicycling advocacy groups that encourage participation. As with many things in Flagstaff, this is part of the fabric of the community that dates back to the pioneer days of the 1890s and, in this case, is the holdover of a nationwide fad that inspired a short-lived yet heroic competition of will and determination.

Bicycling became a popular form of recreation by the 1890s thanks to the advent of pneumatic tires and the improved safety and handling of low-seated "Rover" models as compared to the traditional high-seated "Ordinaries." In the United States, this craze spread from heavily populated eastern cities to frontier towns such as Flagstaff, where local residents could learn about the latest bicycle models by perusing the *Coconino Sun* newspaper. Advertisements from the time describe the Victor Bicycle, which was sold by local agent and lumberman F.W. Sisson, and the "Indestructible Maywood," which was a thirty-pound bicycle with "twenty-eight-inch, one-piece wooden rim wheels" and "best quality piano wire spokes." Replacement wheels could be bought at the Babbitt brothers' store and other merchandisers. Newspaper stories even advised the proper clothing for female riders:

> *There is no reason why the entire world of women cyclers, young and old, shapely and unshapely, lean and fat, handsome and ugly, should not adopt*

the abbreviated skirt and have as good a time as the male patrons of the "bike," who are grossly indifferent as to their looks.[10]

Bicycle enthusiasts were soon meeting and planning trips, and the most notorious was the seventy-mile journey along a road that followed a stagecoach route between the Grand Canyon and Flagstaff. On August 24, 1894, eight riders left Flagstaff at 5:00 a.m. A newspaper's account of the trip stated, "The journey was made over a mountain road and without an accident." Riders arrived at the Grand Canyon between 7:00 and 8:30 p.m and completed the first of four annual cycling trips to the Canyon.

Interest in bicycling continued to grow, and in May 1895, seventeen Flagstaff residents, including members of such prominent families as the Riordans, Brannens and Sissons, joined the League of American Wheelmen, a national organization that promoted bicycling.

On August 22, 1895, five riders made the second organized bicycle trip to the Grand Canyon. The time it took for them to reach the canyon is unknown, but the riders suffered through a rainstorm and muddy road, which added hazards to an already uneven and sometimes poorly-marked pathway. The group explored the Grand Canyon for several days and made the return trip to Flagstaff in seven hours on August 26.

On January 23, 1896, the Coconino Cycling Club became a local force, electing officers, meeting every Monday night in the Bank Hotel and taking

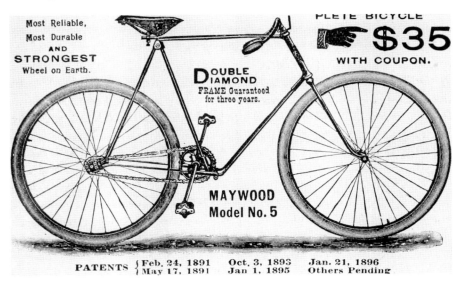

Advertisement for Maywood Bicycle. *Kevin Schindler's collection.*

over the organization of the annual bicycle ride to the Grand Canyon. Meanwhile, businesses continued to adapt their offerings to meet the continued, strong interest in bicycling. In July, the Sykes Brothers—Godfrey and Stanley—installed new machinery in their shop on Leroux Street that allowed them to "make or mend anything" while specializing in guns and bicycles. The "make or mend" description proved to be accurate, and they were able to design and build the birthday cake–like telescope dome that still stands at Lowell Observatory.

Under the sponsorship of the Coconino Bicycling Club, big plans were made for an August 19, 1896 trip to the Grand Canyon. Initially expecting at least one hundred participants, organizers planned to split participants into three groups based on their fitness levels and expected time to reach the Grand Canyon, which ranged from ten-and-a-half to thirteen-and-a-half hours. Meals were available along the trail, and sleeping accommodations were reserved, all for the price of ten dollars per participant. Boosters made souvenir ribbon badges for finishers, and pre-ride activities, held the day before the race, included a visit to cliff dwellings—probably at Walnut Canyon, now a national monument—and a parade.

To the disappointment of organizers, only thirteen riders showed up due to heavy rainstorms. The roads were muddy, and several riders dropped out at the Moqui Stage Station and took a stagecoach for the last fourteen miles. Those seven who finished arrived at the Grand Canyon between 6:00 and 10:00 p.m.; one rider had broken his chain and pushed his bicycle the last fourteen miles. After two days of hiking and cave exploration in the Grand Canyon, the riders returned on August 22 in eight hours.

Despite the poor turnout the previous year, the Coconino Cycling Club optimistically planned a big event for the September 7, 1897 run. As in 1896, they created a lot of publicity. Riders could register for eleven dollars, which covered the cost of sleeping and board at the canyon, meals and transportation of luggage that weighed less than twenty-five pounds. Recommendations suggested that riders have bikes "with gear not exceeding 66, and also with coasters and brake."[11]

While the records of participation in the 1897 event seem to have been lost to history, the turnout was likely uninspiring, as this was the last run to the Grand Canyon organized by the Coconino Cycling Club. Despite the race's short life, it represents an early example of Flagstaff's appreciation for bicycling that helped set the wheels in motion for the community's modern identity as a bicycle-friendly place, and it inspires today's enthusiasts to retrace the steps of these hardy cycling pioneers.

THE WEATHERFORD HOTEL

*O*n a cold, windy night in early April 1920, a twenty-six-year-old woman named Carley stepped off a train in Flagstaff and walked a block west, then north to where she would spend the night at Flagstaff's finest lodge, the Weatherford Hotel. She had traveled from New York on a quest to reconnect with her boyfriend, Glenn, whom she hadn't seen in fifteen months. The last time they had been together wasn't pleasant, and he had recently returned from France, where he suffered from shell shock and gas exposure while serving in World War I. He told Carley he was going to move west to try to recover his health. He ended up in Oak Creek Canyon, twenty miles south of Flagstaff. Then, more than a year later, Carley decided to journey to Arizona to rekindle the couple's relationship. She hadn't told Glenn her plans, so she was especially anxious for the next day when she would ride down to his ranch and surprise him. Would he be pleased or distressed to see her? Was their relationship even salvageable? She reflected on these questions as she settled into her room. She realized that when she left the hotel the next morning, she would be leaving her old life behind and venturing into the future that she hoped would bring the fulfilment of her dreams.

Carley's epiphany at the Weatherford was not unique; generations of people before and since have gone there for inspiration to fulfill their dreams. In fact, the hotel itself exists because of a man who dreamed of leaving his mark on northern Arizona. His name was John Weatherford, and history has shown that he realized his dream. His hotel stands as one of several monuments to his dedication and vision.

John Weatherford was born in Fort Worth, Texas, in 1859. He grew up in the Lone Star State and lived there until the late 1880s. Once he was married, he and his wife, Margaret, moved away and settled in Flagstaff in 1886 or 1887. John quickly involved himself in the community, serving as Justice of the Peace and clerk for the first elected Coconino County Board of Supervisors. He also played an active role in establishing the Northern Arizona Normal School, and he became a charter member of the Elks Club. Weatherford was an entrepreneur and, at one point, purportedly traded his horse and buggy for lots of land downtown where he planned to establish businesses. Three of these were at the southwest corner of Leroux Street and Aspen Avenue.

Around 1897 or 1898, Weatherford built a two-floor structure here. He opened a general store on the ground floor and lived upstairs with his family, but he had grander plans; Weatherford wanted a hotel and restaurant, too. In 1899, he expanded on the original structure to create a stunning facility, which he appropriately named the Weatherford Hotel. The hotel stood three stories high and was built with brick and "Arizona Red" building stone. A balcony wrapped around the upper level of the building, and a distinctive cupola added even more character.

John and Margaret Weatherford at the Weatherford Hotel. *Northern Arizona University, Cline Library, Will Weatherford Collection.*

Weatherford Hotel before the 1929 fire that destroyed the balcony and cupola. *Kevin Schindler's collection.*

Construction proceeded quickly, and with much fanfare, the restaurant opened on December 24, 1899. Dinner was served from 5:30 to 7:30 p.m., and the menu, as reported in the *Coconino Sun*, included appetizers such as raw oysters, cream of chicken à la Reine, baked whitefish à la bordelaise, lobster salad en mayonnaise and boiled Oxford ham with pecan sauce. Entrees included heart of mutton à la petite poise, sauté of beef with dumplings, minced turkey giblets en rice, banana fritters with wine sauce, sirloin of beef au jus and stuffed young turkey with cranberry sauce. For dessert, guests could choose from green apple, mince and pumpkin pie, brandy jelly with whipped cream, boston cream puffs and lemon ice with English fruit cake.[12]

Weatherford opened the hotel itself on January 1, 1900. The structure featured some forty rooms that included the then-modern conveniences of running water, electric lights, heat and a communal bathroom on each floor. By today's standard, a shared bathroom seems inconvenient, but a bathroom on each floor was a valued amenity back then. The basement was also developed for use as a bar. In 1909, Weatherford built another structure just to the south of the hotel in order to house a telephone company. Also built of Arizona Red, it was later converted into a café and the beautiful sandstone covered with a stucco façade. Meanwhile, a 1929 fire destroyed the balcony and cupola of the hotel, but the business was able to continue regular operations. It's a good thing the main hotel structure was built of Arizona Red!

For years, the hotel and restaurant were popular with both tourists and locals. According to hotel records, newspaper magnate William Randolph Hearst, artist Thomas Moran, western legend Wyatt Earp, and other famous people stayed there. William Boyd, who was later a famous actor known as "Hopalong Cassidy," once worked as a clerk there.

By the 1960s, the Weatherford Hotel, like much of downtown Flagstaff, was becoming rundown. The hotel was no longer a preferred destination. At one point, the upper floors were used as a youth hostel, and there was talk of tearing down the entire facility. Then in 1975, the fortunes of the hotel and adjoining café and, in fact, the downtown area in general, changed when it was all sold to a couple who dreamed of bringing the area back to its days of glory. Their names were Henry Taylor and Pamela (Sam) Green, and they invested a lot of time and money in turning the hotel back into a gem of downtown. On the ground floor, they soon opened Charly's Restaurant and Charly's Bar, which were both named after Charly Spining, a local musician of significant repute. In 1995, they removed the façade on the telephone

Lowell Observatory trustee emeritus Bill Putnam drives his great-uncle Percival Lowell's car past the Weatherford Hotel during Flagstaff's annual July Fourth parade in 2014. Mike Kitt is one of the passengers waving a flag from the back seat on the passenger side. *Kevin Schindler's collection.*

Zane Grey and Allen Doyle on a bear hunt in northern Arizona. *Kevin Schindler's collection.*

company-turned café and reopened it as the Exchange Club, a dining area for the adjacent Charly's Restaurant. They converted a section of the third floor into an area called the Zane Grey Ballroom in 1997, and the following year, they reinstalled the upper-level balconies. They also added back a cupola, bringing the exterior back to its original look.

By 1999, the Taylors had achieved their goal of returning the hotel to the former glory that John Weatherford had created. Just like Weatherford had celebrated a new century when he opened the hotel, the Taylors now planned to honor Weatherford and welcome the twenty-first century. They conceived the idea of lowering a pine cone—a localized version of the ball dropping in New York's Times Square—from the corner of the hotel to mark the new year and new century. They built a rustic "pinecone" out of a garbage can, foam wedding cake, some Christmas lights and several real pinecones. At midnight, they lowered it with ropes and pulleys. The event was a big hit amongst the revelers in the streets, and thus began Flagstaff's Annual Pinecone Drop. Every New Year's Eve, thousands of people stuff themselves into winter gear and cram the downtown area to see the pine cone—now a six-foot-tall, seventy-pound apparatus covered with hundreds of metal petals and LED lights—drop at ten o'clock and again at midnight. It's a time of wonder and an opportunity to say goodbye to the past year and look forward to a new year of dreams in the same place that a young lady named Carley dreamed in 1920.

And what became of Carley and Glenn? They got back together and forged a new life. To be clear, their story is fictional. It is an early scene from *Call of the Canyon*, a tale first published in serial form by *The Ladies Home Journal* in 1921 and 1922. It was made into a movie in 1923 and published in book form in 1924. The author was western romance writer Zane Grey, who purportedly composed much of this story and others from the upstairs area of the Weatherford Hotel that is now named the Zane Grey Ballroom.

LEAVE IT AS IT IS

Graduates of Flagstaff High School's Class of 1903—all five of them—had a special reason to be excited on commencement day. The date was May 6, 1903, and the ceremony took place at the Grand Canyon. Graduation was witnessed by three hundred Flagstaff residents who had traveled for two hours early that morning on a train from Flagstaff to the Grand Canyon. Hundreds more people joined the festivities, including territorial officials like Governor Alexander Brodie. Even the Arizona Lumber and Timber Company's band was on hand to provide entertainment throughout the day.

From a hotel balcony, Brodie introduced the guest speaker, who eloquently discussed the virtues of Arizona. After the speech ended, the Flagstaff High School principal presented the students to the guest speaker, who gave each graduate a diploma and some words of encouragement. The class then gave the speaker a Navajo buckskin boot and a poem written by the Coconino County superintendent of schools, Harrison Conrard.

One can only imagine the euphoria the students felt throughout the ceremony, later that day and for the rest of their lives. You only graduate from high school once, and the memories of the occasion stick with you forever—especially when the guest speaker is Theodore Roosevelt, president of the United States.

Roosevelt, who was the first sitting president to visit the Grand Canyon State, didn't travel all the way from Washington, D.C., to Arizona just to pass out diplomas to a handful of students. His stop here was one of dozens

Theodore Roosevelt. *Library of Congress Prints and Photographs Division.*

he made during an eight-week tour of the West. Visiting twenty-five states and a variety of natural wonders such as Yosemite and Yellowstone, he gave a staggering 263 speeches on the trip. For his Grand Canyon presentation, Roosevelt focused on two interests that were close to his heart—irrigation and conservation. Just a year prior, he had signed into law the Newlands Reclamation Act, which funded irrigation efforts in the West. He alluded to this in the concluding sentiments of his speech that still ring true today:

> *It is a pleasure to be in Arizona. I have never been in it before. Arizona is one of the regions from which I expect most development through the wise action of the national congress in passing the irrigation act...I look forward to the effects of irrigation as being of greater consequence to all this region of country in the next fifty years than any other movement whatsoever.*[13]

As for his views on conservation, he couldn't have been in a more appropriate place to convey them. He said:

> *I have come here to see the Grand Canyon of Arizona, because in the canyon Arizona has a natural wonder, which, so far as I know, is in kind absolutely unparalleled throughout the rest of the world. I shall not attempt to describe it, because I cannot. I could not choose the words that would convey to any outsider what the canyon is. I want to ask you to do one thing in connection with it in your own interest and in the interest of the country—to keep this great wonder as it is… Leave it as it is. Man cannot improve on it; not a bit. The ages have been at work on it and man can only mar it. What you can do is to keep it for your children and your children's children and for all who come after you, as one of the great sights which every American, if he can travel at all, should see.*[14]

These irrigation and conservation ideas, and the actions that ensued from them, such as the construction of the Glen Canyon and Hoover Dams, profoundly impacted people across the United States and perhaps nowhere more so than in Arizona. For those five graduating seniors who had front row seats to Roosevelt's inspiring words, the world they were about to enter must have looked full of hope and excitement.

LAKE MARY

*I*n the spring of 1884, a thirty-four-year-old Indian agent at Fort Defiance, Arizona came to Flagstaff to manage a lumber mill. Within three years, he owned the operation and brought his two, younger half-brothers, Michael and Timothy, from Chicago to help him run it. His name was Denis "Matt" Riordan, and the contributions he and his family made to the development of Flagstaff were crucial and far-reaching. For years, their company, the Arizona Lumber and Timber Company, was the largest employer in Flagstaff, but they did so much more than just supply jobs. Related to the Babbitt brothers by marriage (Michael and Timothy had married sisters, Elizabeth and Caroline Metz of Cincinnati, who were cousins of the Babbitts), they were community builders of the first order and spearheaded efforts to establish medical, educational and religious amenities. They played key roles in establishing Coconino County and making electricity available community wide. They also helped meet Flagstaff's water needs by creating a reservoir a dozen miles southeast of downtown. Called Lake Mary, it has not only supplied water for everyday living for more than a century, but it has also served as a major recreation area for boaters, anglers and adventurers who kick off each new year by jumping into the lake's frigid waters.

Flagstaff was settled in 1876 but began to grow in earnest after the railroad arrived in the summer of 1882. Initially, residents gathered water from a spring at the original townsite, which is located a mile west of modern downtown and is referred to as "Old Town." Residents also found a few other springs around town, but these could not supply enough water when more people—and businesses—arrived. In the late 1890s, community leaders, such as Julius Aubineau, began developing the Inner Basin Pipeline, which brought water from springs in the San Francisco Peaks to a 2.5-million-gallon reservoir located some three miles northwest of downtown, along modern-day Schultz Pass Road. From the reservoir, another pipe carried water to town. This system was adequate for domestic use, but the Riordans' mill required much more water than it could supply. By this time, Matt had left town, but Michael and Tim were still running the company and leading efforts to improve the pipeline.

While these improvements were being made, Tim was also scoping out other possible water sources. One of these was a valley ten miles southeast of downtown. It didn't actually have water in it at the time, but Tim thought its shape would be conducive to holding water if it was dammed up. It was located in an area called Clark's Valley, which was named after one of Flagstaff's founding fathers, John Clark. Clark came to northern Arizona in the spring of 1876 with fellow sheepherder William Henry Ashurst. It was during this trip that future U.S. Senator Henry Fountain Ashurst was born. While the Ashursts settled by a spring on Anderson Mesa about one mile east of present-day Ashurst Lake, Clark set up a ranch just south of Anderson Mesa in what was soon called Clark's Valley.

A small stream, Walnut Creek, ran through Clark's Valley. While the stream didn't provide a lot of water, Tim thought that a dam might pool the water in the valley. In 1897, after a rancher had experimented with a small dam, Tim arranged for an eight-foot-high earthen dam to be constructed. In 1904, the Riordans received permission from the federal government to build a more substantial structure. This resulted in a nearly forty-foot-high dam; it soon formed a reservoir that Tim named Lake Mary, after his eldest daughter. This water was then piped to town for both commercial and public use.

The dam proved unsatisfactory over time, because the water source, Walnut Creek, was intermittent. Problems also arose when the water in Lake Mary slowly drained off through sinkholes in the underlying limestone. Finally, in 1941, Flagstaff leaders built a second, taller dam to the south of Lake Mary, and it formed a new reservoir that was called Upper Lake Mary while the original reservoir became known as Lower Lake Mary. Upper Lake Mary was able to reliably gather—and hold—much more water than Lower Lake Mary. The new dam was raised another ten feet in 1951 in order to maximize its holding capacity. While Lower Lake Mary often dries up, save

Boaters aboard *The White Rose of Lake Mary*. *Northern Arizona University, Cline Library, NAU General Photograph Collection.*

Modern view of Lake Mary with San Francisco Peaks in the background. *Kevin Schindler's collection.*

for a few small pools, it can still fill its entire three-mile length. The upper lake never dries up and can reach a length of five miles.

While Tim Riordan created the original Lake Mary as a water source, he was also quite interested in using it for recreation. He loved to fish and sail, and he could often be seen enjoying these pastimes on the lake. Modern recreationists continue this tradition. On any given day, anglers can be found on Upper Lake Mary trying to catch northern pike, walleye, bass, catfish, crappie and other stocked fish. They often have to negotiate around water skiers, swimmers, motorboats and other water craft that are also on the lake. People also fish in Lower Lake Mary, but its overall recreational use is limited. Campers and nature watchers also gather around the lakes to enjoy the freshness of the outdoors and watch birds, elk and other wildlife. Then there are those brave souls who gather at noon every January 1 and jump, perhaps while they are not thinking clearly due to New Year's Eve partying, into Upper Lake Mary's icy waters for the "Randy Wilson Memorial Flagstaff Polar Plunge."

The lakes encompass a truly unique heritage that ranges from long-ago ranching and milling to the construction of dams that supply water for daily living and recreation. Walking their shores hints at much of this legacy—an early fence post or dam material here, an errant fish hook and leftover tent stake there—and serves as a reminder of Tim Riordan's vision of Lake Mary. Of the many contributions he made to the Flagstaff community, he considered the creation of Lake Mary to be his greatest.[15]

LAVA RIVER CAVE

*A*s pioneers made their way to Flagstaff in the late nineteenth and early twentieth centuries, they faced challenges typical of those who tried to settle the frontier. They had to build shelters that would adequately protect them from extreme variations in weather, they had to figure out how to obtain regular supplies of food and water and they had to fight off sickness. They often had to do without many of the comforts and conveniences that people in more developed areas took for granted. Cold drinks and refrigerated food storage, for instance, were luxuries, so one can only imagine the thrill these pilgrims must have felt when they stumbled across the entrance to a cave that was thick with ice in the woods twenty miles north of town. They found that the ice often remained year-round, which meant they had means of chilling their food and drinks. They also discovered that the cave was not a typical cavity formed by pockets of dissolved limestone, but rather it was the result of flowing lava. Thus arose the name Lava River Cave for this ¾-mile-long subterranean feature of the San Francisco Volcanic Field, an 1,800-square-mile stretch of landscape across northern Arizona.

The San Francisco Volcanic Field consists of some six hundred volcanoes that are the result of volcanic activity that occurred between six million and one thousand years ago. The oldest of these volcanoes formed near present-day Williams. Through the years, additional volcanoes have formed in a continuously-migrating, eastern direction. The most dominant of the volcanoes is the stratovolcano remnant known today as the San

Icy entrance to Lava River Cave. *Kevin Schindler's collection.*

Francisco Peaks. The youngest volcano in the field is Sunset Crater, whose eruption around one thousand years ago was likely witnessed by Puebloans living nearby.

Evidence of this ancient geological turmoil includes not only the volcanoes themselves, but also lava tubes like Lava River Cave. The cave's origins date back about seven hundred thousand years, when a volcano erupted near today's Hart Prairie on the western side of the San Francisco Peaks. As the lava flowed downhill, the sides and top of the flow, which were in contact with the colder ground and air, cooled and formed a crust while the molten rock inside the flow continued to move through a conduit. Eventually, the source of the lava was cut off, but the internal flow continued until the conduit was drained, leaving a long cavity known as a lava tube. The entire process of formation probably occurred within a few hours, which is very fast in geological terms.

Lava tubes are found around the world in areas where volcanic activity has been present. Scientists also believe they have detected evidence of lava tubes on the Moon and perhaps planets and other moons in the solar system. Photographs of the lunar surface document numerous, long, narrow channels known as rilles. One of these, Hadley Rille, was explored by Apollo 15 astronauts Dave Scott and Jim Irwin, who carried out much of their geological training for this work in the San Francisco Volcanic Field. Some of these lunar rilles were likely created by the collapse of lava tube roofs that had previously been formed.

For years, Lava River Cave was known as Government Cave because of its proximity to nearby Government Prairie. Historic evidence suggests that Government Prairie was so-named because it was a location for military personnel stationed in Prescott to pasture their horses in the summer.

Scientists like Harold Colton, founder of the Museum of Northern Arizona, saw the cave as a natural laboratory for deciphering the nature of such features. They determined that the entrance was created by the collapse of a section of the tube's ceiling. The collapse resulted in an opening that descended steeply amid fallen rocks before flattening out. This cave served as a portal for not only human explorers, but for bats, raccoons and other forest inhabitants looking for shelter as well. The coolest temperature in the tube is at the entrance where it is thirty-five degrees fahrenheit year-round.

Gretchen Schindler inside Lava River Cave. *Kevin Schindler's collection.*

Often, the temperature in the cave is cold enough for seeping water to freeze, which meant there were icicles and blocks of ice that the pioneers were able to mine. Because of this tendency for frozen deposits, lava tubes are sometimes called "ice caves." In the winter months, cold air enters the tube and sinks to the bottom. The dark basaltic rocks are good insulators and help keep the temperature cold even in the summer months.

The Lava River Cave has a maximum ceiling height of thirty feet. Several distinct features help tell the story of the cavity's formation. Just after the tube flattens out, small (one-quarter-inch or smaller) "lavasicles" are visible on the ceiling. After the rock had solidified, a later blast of heat from the volcano caused some of the rock to liquefy and drip. Farther back in the tube is an area where lava flowed on both sides of an obstruction. This feature is frozen in time and serves as an indicator of the direction of lava flow. Throughout the cave are splashdowns, which are rocks that fell from the recently hardened ceiling and walls into the still-molten lava on the floor. The lava then cooled and permanently trapped the fallen rocks. Cooling cracks are also easily visible throughout the tube. These are found near the intersection of the walls and floor that formed during cooling of the lava. They are often several inches thick and may extend from a few inches to tens of feet long.

While the original pioneers mined the cave for its riches of ice and later scientists studied it for the treasure of knowledge, the cave quickly became a recreation destination. It is an element of the area's tourism industry that continues to bring visitors from around the world.

GRAND FALLS

In a critical scene from the 1964 movie *A Distant Trumpet*, Cavalry Lieutenant Matthew Hazard (played by Troy Donahue) travels to Mexico to try and convince the Chiricahua Apache chief, War Eagle, to surrender and agree to move his people to a reservation in Arizona. The backdrop of this exchange is a picturesque waterfall with chocolate brown water cascading over a series of ledges. Northern Arizonans might recognize this waterfall, because it is not really in Mexico. Rather, it is in a spot thirty miles northeast of Flagstaff and is known as Grand Falls.

Millennia before Warner Bros. filmed *A Distant Trumpet*, the forces of nature created Grand Falls as the result of volcanic activity in the San Francisco Volcanic Field. On the eastern side of this expanse lies a cinder cone known as Merriam Crater, which was named after naturalist Clinton Hart Merriam. Thousands of years ago (the exact timing has been debated by scientists for years) a fissure opened in Merriam Crater or in a smaller nearby crater. Hot lava poured out and flowed downhill in a northeasterly direction. After running for about seven miles, the lava coursed into a two-hundred-foot-deep channel of the Little Colorado River. The lava filled the channel and overflowed to the northeast for a half mile, resulting in a natural basalt dam after the lava hardened. When river water arrived at the dam, it pooled up until it diverted around the northeast side of the barrier. It eventually reentered its original channel, spilling over the rocks to form the Grand Falls. The russet hue of the water, due to suspended silt, gave rise to the nickname "Chocolate Falls."

Diagram showing how the Little Colorado River was diverted around the volcanic deposit and cascaded over the cliff to form Grand Falls. *From Harold Colton and Frank Baxter's "Days in the Painted Desert and the San Francisco Mountains: A Guide," 1927.*

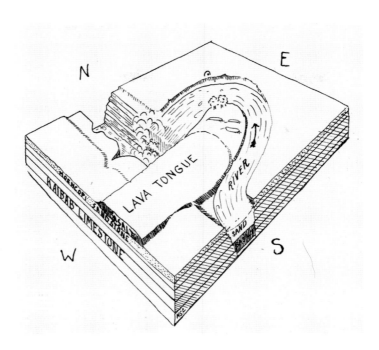

Cascade of the Little Colorado. From Lorenzo Sitgreaves's "Report of an Expedition down the Zuni and Colorado Rivers," 1853.

Modern view of Grand Falls. *Michael Collier*.

Since the falls formed, the relentless flow of water has eroded the underlying Kaibab Limestone, resulting in a stair-stepped rock wall over which the water cascades. With a vertical drop of 185 feet, Grand Falls is taller than Niagara Falls.

For years, Navajos watered their sheep here and early white trappers and hunters in the area also likely knew about Grand Falls, but the first white person to describe them was explorer Lorenzo Sitgreaves. In early October 1851, his expedition reached Grand Falls, and Sitgreaves noted:

> *October 8, Camp No. 14—About a mile below the last camp the river falls over a succession of horizontal ledges of sandstone, forming a beautiful cascade of one hundred to one hundred twenty feet in vertical height, and continues on its course through a canyon of that depth, the general level of the banks remaining the same. Having been informed by my guide (Antoine Leroux) and other experienced trappers that this canyon extends down the river to its junction with the Colorado, and the great canyon through which the latter flows, I regarded the attempt to follow the river to its mouth as too hazardous, considering the condition of the animals, and the state of the supplies, and therefore, by advice of the guide, turned off towards the mountains, with the purpose of striking the Colorado below the great canon,*

and then exploring it upward as far as might be found practicable. Leaving the river, then, we passed along the base of high table lands, the lava sand lying several inches deep upon the ground....[16]

While Sitgreaves didn't find the water route for which he searched, he did bring attention to these breathtaking falls. Today, hikers, photographers and other outdoor enthusiasts enjoy exploring Grand Falls. Most especially enjoy going in springtime, when the melted snow upstream gushes through the river channel and cascades to the rocks below, just as it did in *A Distant Trumpet.*

THE ORPHEUM THEATRE

*F*lagstaff has had its share of opera houses, movie theaters, dance halls and other entertainment venues through the years, but only one has stood the test of time and endures as an icon of Flagstaff's vibrant downtown landscape. Located on the site of a former chicken yard, the Orpheum Theatre's presence—one might say its personality—is one that triggers even the casual visitor to utter, "If only these walls could talk." For a century, it has been a center for the performing and cinematic arts in Flagstaff.

The Orpheum traces its history back to Flagstaff pioneer and community builder John Weatherford. After Weatherford opened his hotel at the corner of Aspen Avenue and Leroux Street on January 1, 1900, he soon looked to make use of the empty lot to the west. Responding to his customers' yearning for fresh eggs, he erected an eight-foot-high fence around the lot and ran a chicken farm. According to Flagstaff historian Joe Meehan, this venture was short-lived, "Weatherford found out you had to heat chickens in the winter, and so he had a sale on chicken dinners and that was the end of the chicken yard."[17]

A decade later, Weatherford conceived another use for the site, one that would endure much longer than a chicken farm. Movies were becoming wildly popular at the time, and he decided to capitalize on this craze by building Flagstaff's first dedicated cinema house. Weatherford opened the Majestic Theatre on October 27, 1911, and formed a team that, by 1913, consisted of John Costigan and Lee Smith. Business was good until December 31, 1915, when a heavy storm dumped five feet of snow on Flagstaff and resulted in the collapse of the Majestic and other buildings.

Weatherford planned to rebuild the theater, but Costigan and Smith didn't want to wait for this to happen. They preferred to keep the operation running, so they rented space in the McMillan Building, which was a block south of Weatherford's hotel, as a temporary location for the Majestic. They began showing movies just a week after the storm and continued doing so for several weeks. Costigan soon bought out Smith and found a larger, more permanent site: the Babbitts' old garage, which was located on the present site of Heritage Square. On this site on March 3, 1916, he opened the new Empress Theatre.

The following month, Weatherford began work on his own, new theatre, which was much larger than the original Majestic. Since Costigan had taken the name with him and used it while operating at the McMillan Building, Weatherford needed a new name for his theater and chose Orpheum, after the Greek musician and poet.

Some of the details of the Orpheum's history get a little hazy at this point, with some reports indicating the grand opening was on August 3, 1917. However, in keeping with the tradition of many western tales, this does not appear to be accurate. Newspaper accounts from the time show that, under the management of John Barncord, the Orpheum opened on August 31, 1916, and was hosting regular programming by October. According to a story in the August 25, 1916 edition of the *Coconino Sun*, as Barncord readied to open the Orpheum, he said, "The new show house is one of the best and most complete for its size in the southwest, with a capacity that will answer for time to come."[18]

For the next several months, the Orpheum and Empress competed for business, with each advertising programs in the *Coconino Sun*. The Orpheum, which seated twice as many as the 350-seat Empress, eventually won out. On August 4, 1917, John Costigan purchased the lease from Barncord to operate the Orpheum and, at the same time, closed the Empress.

The ensuing century proved Barncord's words were prescient, and the Orpheum's capacity certainly answered for some time to come. Movies, plays and musical performances were augmented by fundraisers, war bond sales and other community-centered activities. For years, these efforts were driven by Costigan's sister, Mary, who initially helped John run the operation but eventually took over management when his health failed.

Mary was a gifted promoter and woman of many talents. In the mid-1920s, she became the first female licensed radio broadcaster in Arizona and, according to some reports, in the nation. She set up the radio station KFXY in the Orpheum, and on December 10, 1925, Flagstaff's first radio program was broadcast.

Orpheum Theatre. *Kevin Schindler's collection.*

This tradition of entertainment and community-centered activity continued at the Orpheum through 1999, when, to the dismay of many residents, it closed. The facility remained closed for three years until Chris Scully entered the picture. Scully recalled that, by that point in his life, he had seen some 120 Grateful Dead rock-and-roll concerts, as well as another 500 performances by other bands.[19] He had also spearheaded Flagstaff's New Year's Eve and New Millennium celebration just as the Orpheum was closing. He was a man who was clearly passionate about music, and in 2002, he partnered with Turney Postlewait, Art Babbott and Neil Nepksy to lease the Orpheum and reopen it as an entertainment venue.

The Orpheum's tradition as a premiere entertainment venue and as a site for hosting fundraisers was able to continue. In this new era, these efforts resulted in hundreds of thousands of dollars for everything from relief for the victims of Hurricane Katrina and several natural disasters in Haiti to the Hometown Heroes benefit in support of humanitarian efforts in Nicaragua and a local suicide prevention program called We Care.

Another fundraiser held at the Orpheum, for Lowell Observatory, featured Alan Stern, who was the principal investigator of the New Horizons mission that flew by Pluto in 2015. The Orpheum was chosen as the site for the event

Kevin Schindler, Charlene Christy, Jim Christy and Alan Stern give a "Pluto Salute" (nine fingers held up to represent nine planets, supporting the idea that Pluto should properly be called a planet) during a 2015 Lowell Observatory fundraiser at the Orpheum. *Kevin Schindler's collection.*

because it was here, on February 18, 1930, that Clyde Tombaugh watched Gary Cooper star in the movie *The Virginian* just hours after Tombaugh had discovered Pluto at Lowell Observatory.

A century of entertainment, fundraisers, radio broadcasts and celebrations—that's quite a history for a site that started out as a chicken yard.

THE MUSEUM OF NORTHERN ARIZONA

*O*ne of Flagstaff's valued research institutions, the Museum of Northern Arizona, came into existence, in large part, due to the efforts of a husband-and-wife team. Harold Sellers Colton, a professional zoologist, was born in 1881 and grew up in Philadelphia. He earned his PhD from the University of Pennsylvania in 1908. Brought up as a gentleman in a wealthy family in Quaker Pennsylvania, Colton commissioned a sailing ship, the *Clione*, and happily sailed up and down the East Coast pursuing his interests. He also taught introductory zoology courses at his alma mater. Although satisfied with his life, he showed few signs of becoming one of America's leading zoologists. Harold could have become a member of the Philadelphia elite, but being a nonconformist, he was not interested in pursuing that lifestyle.

Colton met the beautiful and vivacious Mary-Russell Ferrell and, in short order, married her in 1912. Born in Kentucky, Ferrell was an outsider to Philadelphia high society, but she succeeded in making a modest living as an accomplished artist. It is evident that she had a profound influence on the more modest Harold, because he soon sold his boat and embarked on a journey in new intellectual directions. The Coltons had spent their honeymoon in the Flagstaff area in 1912. Four years later, they returned to Flagstaff for the summer and became interested in the local Native American ruins, and the two soon published an article about them. Within a few years, Harold authored a brilliant theoretical model interpreting the site-distribution data using the life-zone concept previously developed by zoologist C. Hart Merriam.

Flagstaff, being located on the slope of a volcanic mountain, has extreme elevation gradients that are duplicated in very few places. This has made the area a unique living laboratory for biological and ecological studies. In the early part of the twentieth century, Merriam had noted that this elevation gradient resulted in wetter conditions upslope and drier conditions downslope, and it is what makes the Flagstaff area a pine forest "island" in the midst of arid desert. Plants in the area are segregated into associations driven by moisture levels that Merriam called "life zones." The Coltons seized on this idea and realized that populations of animals and humans tended to move upslope when conditions became drier and downslope when conditions were more wet. This was one of the first theoretical models, later developed by numerous researchers, in southwestern archaeology.

The Coltons spent their summers in northern Arizona pursuing their new interests and developing many friendships there. In 1926, the year after Harold's father died, the couple and their son moved permanently to Flagstaff. Like many others before and since, the Coltons moved to the American West to reinvent themselves and to seek new opportunities and challenges. The following year, they gained the title to the old McMillan homestead. Thomas McMillan is considered by many historians as Flagstaff's first permanent white settler; he owned a 160-acre spread, and in 1886, he built a house that stills stands across the street from today's Museum of Northern Arizona visitor center. Flagstaff, at the time, was a village of slightly more than five thousand people, but it was already the host of several scientific institutions and the Arizona State Teacher's College.

Led by Grady Gammage, the then-president of the Arizona State Teacher's College, the Flagstaff intellectual community formed the Northern Arizona Society of Science and Art. This society had the central purpose of founding a museum. The Coltons assumed leadership roles in that organization: Harold as director and president of the board and Mary-Russell as the first curator of art and ethnology. Against the wishes and advice of President Gammage, Mrs. Colton wrote passionately to the *Coconino Sun*, the local newspaper, to recommend that the museum should not be part of the college. Mrs. Colton preferred a location with a view of the San Francisco Peaks rather than one "overlooking the unsightly outskirts of town."

Mary-Russell's first preference for the museum's location was on Knob Hill, which is the site of today's Flagstaff Medical Center. However, the museum was forced to start out in two rooms of the Women's Club, which was located in a brick building on Aspen Street where Wheeler Park was

Harold and Mary-Russell Ferrell Colton. *Northern Arizona University, Cline Library, Fronske Studio Collection.*

later developed. On September 6, 1928, the Museum of Northern Arizona first opened its doors to the public in its modest facilities. The rooms were so small that some artifacts had to be stored at the Hotel Monte Vista. In 1935, the museum moved north to its present location that is adjacent to the Rio de Flag on the McMillan homestead and has majestic views of the San Francisco Peaks.

Many of the early Museum of Northern Arizona board members were the stuff of Flagstaff legends. They included Grady Gammage; Timothy Riordan, president of the Arizona Lumber & Timber Co. and friend of explorer John Wesley Powell; Vesto Slipher, director of Lowell Observatory and discoverer of the expanding nature of the universe; Louisa Wetherill, a trader highly revered by the Navajo and married to the legendary explorer John Wetherill, who called her *ne-he-zen-ie* or "our guardian mother"; Andrew Douglass, an astronomer at the University of Arizona, who, as noted earlier, helped found Lowell Observatory and pioneered the scientific method of tree-ring dating; Carl Lampland, a longtime astronomer at Lowell Observatory; and many others who are now synonymous with Flagstaff history.

In the decades since the Museum of Northern Arizona was founded, its staff has carried out numerous significant research projects. The museum has benefited from the leadership of many excellent directors like Edward "Ned" Danson, who served in this capacity for nearly two decades. During that time, he and his family—including his son, future actor Ted Danson— lived in the McMillan house that the Coltons had purchased years before. The museum now houses extensive collections that encompass anthropology, botany, biology, geology, paleontology and zoology, as well as numerous works of fine art, including those created by the many talented Native American artists of the Colorado Plateau. It annually hosts festivals that focus on the artistry and cultural traditions of the Hopi, Zuni and Navajo tribes, as well as a colorful *Celebraciones de la Gente* event.

The Hotel Monte Vista

*W*hile 1927 is remembered as the year Lindbergh flew across the Atlantic and Babe Ruth stormed the sports world by hitting sixty home runs for the New York Yankees, in Flagstaff, a grand community hotel opened thanks to the boosterism and enthusiasm of local citizens.

For years, Flagstaff community leaders envisioned a modern hotel that would meet the needs of both locals and visitors to the area. In August 1925, an eight-person committee that included Lowell Observatory's E.C. Slipher, met with the Hockenberry System Inc. of Pennsylvania to look into the possibility of selling stock to build a new facility. After some research, Hockenberry reported that about $140,000 could be raised by the sale of stock in Flagstaff and that the community could maintain a seventy-room hotel costing up to $250,000. Encouraged by these findings, the committee retained Hockenberry to organize the stock sales.

In April 1926, representatives of Hockenberry set up an office in Flagstaff and prepared for the fundraising campaign, which officially began May 10, 1926. About seventy community members, who were split into twelve groups, aggressively and enthusiastically raised funds. Boosterism was at an all-time high, and the town would host high-spirited luncheons that featured entertainment and songs that often carried out into the streets. A couple examples include:

Fellows, I have just been thinking,
To the world I want to tell,

How our men are all determined,
For to build a new hotel;
We have highways, we have spirits,
We have everything that's swell;
We have scenery, we have climate—
Soon we'll have a new hotel

This one is to the tune of "Battle Hymn of the Republic":

We're out to boost the new hotel
We'll boost it far and near.
We want it here in Flagstaff
We'll get it never fear,
When it comes to boosting,
Opposition has to go;
We're out to get the money and we'll bring in all the dough.

Chorus
Glory, glory, it's for Flagstaff
Glory, glory, it's for Flagstaff
Glory, glory, it's for Flagstaff
We're out to get the money and we'll bring in all the dough.[20]

More than 450 individuals and companies bought stock, including the Babbitts, Riordans, Sliphers and other leading families. In the seven-day campaign, more than $200,000 was raised, enabling the financial success of the venture.

Meanwhile, the original committee of eight, supplemented by the addition of several more people, hired the H.L. Stevens Company of Chicago and San Francisco to build the hotel under the direction of Clark Gramling. The group considered five sites for the new hotel before finally choosing a spot at the northeast corner of San Francisco Street and Aspen Avenue. Under the guise of the "Flagstaff Community Hotel Company," they purchased the entire block, including vacant land and existing buildings, from owners David Babbitt, Tim Riordan and F.S. Breen. The buildings included those previously occupied by the post office and *Coconino Sun*.

Construction of the four-story, seventy-three-room structure began on June 8, 1926, and proceeded at a brisk pace. The subcontractors were Wilson and Coffin of Flagstaff, and with a crew sometimes as large as seventeen, they installed the plumbing. Gramling and his team designed a class B (fireproof) structure and guaranteed the construction cost at $175,600.

The committee held a contest amongst all stockholders to come up with a permanent name for the hotel. Among the dozens of suggestions, one popular choice was *La Bandera* (Spanish for "the Flag"). But in the end, this name was not used due to the concerns of confusing the name with other words such as "bandit." On August 19, 1926, representatives from the hotel committee, the Flagstaff Women's Club and the Business and Professional Women's Club settled on a name submitted by shoe shop owner Loren Savage—Hotel Monte Vista (Spanish for "Mountain View").

At a total cost of $260,000, the hotel was finished sixty days ahead of schedule. On December 31, 1926, the *Coconino Sun* proclaimed, "The Hotel Monte Vista, Flagstaff's new community hotel, stands as an expression of the confidence of Flagstaff citizens in the future of this city and as a monument to their public spirit and civic enterprise." Stockholders enjoyed a sneak preview on January 1, 1927, and the hotel officially opened for business the following day.

Construction of the Hotel Monte Vista in 1926. *Arizona Historical Society, Flagstaff, Blanche Riordan Chambers Collection.*

Modern view of Monte Vista Hotel. *Kevin Schindler's collection.*

True to the expectations of supporters, the "Monte V" grew into an icon of downtown Flagstaff. Opened at the height of prohibition, its cocktail lounge was Flagstaff's first speakeasy. Mary Costigan moved Flagstaff's first radio station, KFXY, from the Orpheum Theatre to the Monte Vista in 1929. The hotel served as a beacon, not only for radio broadcasts, but also for emergency awareness, with a light mounted on the roof flashing as an emergency signal to warn community members of crises. As seems inevitable with a hotel that has been around for decades, the Monte Vista has its share of ghost stories, from a phantom bellboy knocking on guests' doors to a gossamer couple dancing in the lounge.

Perhaps the most striking part of the hotel's history is the collection of Hollywood stars and other luminaries who have stayed there, particularly during the 1940s and 1950s, when producers made dozens of films in the area. Hotel records list among its guests John Wayne, Gary Cooper, Jane Russell, Spencer Tracy, Debbie Reynolds, Bing Crosby, Humphrey Bogart, Bob Hope, Clark Gable and Jane Russell. More contemporary entertainers who have also purportedly stayed at the Monte Vista include Air Supply, Jon Bon Jovi and Freddie Mercury.

As with the predictable emergence of ghost stories through the years, the tales of famous guests have likewise evolved to tall-tale status, which brings to mind a classic line from the movie *The Man Who Shot Liberty Valance*. In the film, when a newspaper editor realizes that Senator Stoddard's reputation is based on a myth, he throws interview notes into a fire and says, "This is the West, sir. When the legend becomes fact, print the legend." In this case, Flagstaff has an example of the "George Washington slept here" myth. For years, the Monte Vista published a brochure listing its many celebrity guests. In addition to the several listed above, another that made the list was Theodore Roosevelt, the intrepid Rough Rider and president who died in 1919—eight years before the hotel opened.

While Roosevelt is, sadly, no longer listed on brochures, the Monte Vista continues to thrive as a monument, not only to public spirit and civic enterprise, but also to community memories and traditions.

WEATHERFORD ROAD

A decade into the twentieth century, John Weatherford had already made quite a name for himself in Flagstaff by building a hotel and theater while also serving the community in other capacities. He was still reaching for the sky with another lofty project, one that climbed into the majestic San Francisco Peaks.

Inspired by construction of a toll road built up Pike's Peak as part of a national movement toward automobile travel during the previous decade, Weatherford applied to the U.S. Forest Service for a permit to build and maintain a fourteen-mile scenic toll road from Fort Valley Road to the top of the San Francisco Peaks on May 28, 1915. He envisioned the toll road as an attraction for tourists and sightseers. The road would also act as an easy access point for firefighters in the event of a fire on the Peaks. Weatherford suggested placing buildings along the path that could house telescopes, refreshments and overnight accommodations. Years later, he proposed selling gasoline and photographs at the toll station/entrance. However, these ideas never came to fruition; Weatherford had his hands full just trying to get the road built.

One thing in Weatherford's favor was the widespread community support. On October 4, 1915, the Common Council of the Town of Flagstaff endorsed the road and thanked Weatherford for spearheading the effort. Several months later, on April 17, 1916, the Coconino County Board of Supervisors also signed off on the idea and sent a declaration of support to the secretary of the Department of Agriculture, because, as today, the management of the Forest Service then fell within this department. The declaration read:

> *First, that we do earnestly recommend the building of a toll road from a point three miles north of Flagstaff, on the Fort Valley Road, to or near the summit of the San Francisco Mountains, proposed by Mr. John W. Weatherford. Second, we believe that this road will be of material benefit to everyone in Arizona, and especially to the citizens of Flagstaff, and will not be detrimental to anyone. Third, any assistance we may be able to render, either morally or otherwise, in the building of said road can be depended upon.*[21]

Thanks to this support, the Forest Service authorized the permit on May 9, 1916. It would terminate after fifty years and it could be cancelled at any time if certain stipulations were not met. Among other conditions, the permit required that construction be completed within two years and the road was to be maintained and kept in a safe, usable state. Initial specifications called for a maximum grade of 7 percent, a fourteen-foot minimum width from shoulder to shoulder and drainage ditches. The permit was originally made out to Weatherford, but it was later transferred to the San Francisco Mountain Scenic Boulevard Company, which Weatherford incorporated on April 13, 1917, for three hundred thousand shares at one dollar per share (about half of these shares were never purchased).

Work on the road, dubbed the San Francisco Mountain Boulevard or simply the Weatherford Road, was hindered from the beginning. Shortages of money, inconsistent labor, poor weather and the demands of World War I slowed and sometimes suspended construction. In 1918, at the urging

This page, top: Postcard of San Francisco Mountain Boulevard entrance and gatehouse. *Kevin Schindler's collection.*

This page, bottom: Entrance to the San Francisco Mountain Boulevard. *Northern Arizona University, Cline Library, Will Weatherford Collection.*

Opposite: Construction of the San Francisco Mountain Boulevard. *Northern Arizona University, Cline Library, Will Weatherford Collection.*

of Senator Henry Fountain Ashurst, the first of several permit extensions was granted. The better part of a decade would pass before the road was ready to be used. Finally, Weatherford and his supporters planned a grand opening for August 15, 1926. More than six hundred visitors in two hundred cars traversed the roughly ten miles of completed road to Fremont Saddle. Festivities included laudatory speeches by Governor George Hunt, Senator Carl Hayden, Flagstaff Chamber of Commerce Vice-President A.J. Mackey and Weatherford.

The road proved to be moderately popular with tourists and even played an important role in scientific research. Years earlier, in 1908 and 1909, Lowell Observatory astronomer Vesto Melvin Slipher climbed into the San Francisco Peaks to observe Mars and to see if he could detect water vapor or oxygen on that planet. Slipher targeted the Peaks, because the obscuring effects of the Earth's atmosphere are reduced in higher elevations. Spurred by the opening of the Weatherford Road in 1926, Slipher returned to the Peaks for more observing. On October 29, he led a team that drove observing equipment and building material up the road to Fremont Saddle. From there, they loaded the gear onto mules and hauled it up Schultz Peak. On top of this peak, they built a roll-off-roof structure that housed a fifteen-inch, reflecting telescope. A unique feature of this housing structure was the use of sawed-off tree stumps as piers to hold the telescope mount.

Located at an elevation of about 11,500 feet, the station was purportedly the highest astronomical observing station in the world at the time. Slipher used it to study planetary atmospheres, the aurora borealis and other celestial features. Another structure was later added and used for a short time by astronomers from Cornell and Harvard Universities to study meteors. The site ultimately proved inadequate for regular observing because of the often-harsh weather conditions and remoteness of the area. The site was abandoned in 1936. One of the stumps used as a pier remains, nearly a century later, and the base of one of the buildings has been rebuilt over the years by hikers and is now used as a shelter.

As for the road, it never turned a profit for Weatherford, and in 1929, he estimated that $130,000 had been spent on construction and upkeep. Unfortunately, the $1-per-car toll didn't cover the costs of maintenance. Weatherford died in 1934 before realizing financial success from the project or seeing the completion of the road to the summit of Humphrey's Peak. The San Francisco Mountain Scenic Boulevard Company marginally continued to operate the road, but the loose road surface quickly deteriorated, and in 1938, the Forest Service terminated the permit due to

Modern view of Weatherford Trail following the pathway of the San Francisco Mountain Boulevard. *Kevin Schindler's collection.*

the lack of maintenance. It was not until 1942 that Congress appropriated $15,500 to the company as compensation for its interests in the road.

While the San Francisco Mountain Scenic Boulevard was short-lived, Weatherford's vision of it as a recreational pathway proved prophetic. The original path of the road was used as the basis for the Weatherford Trail, which has become a popular hiking path. This trail, along with the tollhouse, which remains on the land as a private residence, immortalizes the man who reached for the sky.

WILSON RILES

*B*y the early 1920s, a decade before Clyde Tombaugh commenced his planet search, Flagstaff's K-12 education system had matured to a point where classes were being taught at several primary schools, a high school and at the Northern Arizona Normal School. It would seem that the educational needs of the area were being met, but this changed in 1925 when the Arizona legislature required that black students be segregated. When an attempt to simply put black students into separate rooms didn't satisfy the law, local officials planned to place a new school on Flagstaff's south side, which was where most of the black families lived. According to local educator Bill Cummings, it was called the Colored School and began operating in 1925 with Effie Autry as the first teacher. A new building was soon constructed, and in 1927, the facility was renamed the Dunbar School in honor of Paul Lawrence Dunbar of Dayton, Ohio, the son of former slaves and a classmate of the famous aviator Orville Wright. Dunbar only lived to the age of thirty-three, but he left an important mark as one of the first prominent black poets.

Cleo Wilson began teaching at the school in 1926, and she soon married and became Cleo Wilson Murdoch. In 1929, she took on the duties of being a principal and continued to serve in this dual role until her death in 1940. Later principals included Louise Phillips (1940–42), Annetta Smith (1942–46) and Wilson Riles (1946–54). Riles, in particular, played a key role in Flagstaff history, and his Abraham Lincoln–like story of rising from humble beginnings is an inspiration to locals.

Wilson Riles was born in a small, rural Louisiana town in 1917 to a poor family that soon orphaned him. He was left with family friends Leon and Narvia Bryant, who stepped in to raise him. Riles sold milk to support himself, and with financial help from his church, he was able to attend high school in New Orleans. After graduating in 1936, he moved with his adoptive family to Flagstaff, where Leon went to work at the Cady Lumber Company.

Wilson wanted to attend college, but he would need a job to pay for courses. As a newcomer to town, he didn't know where to start looking for work, so he consulted Cleo Murdoch, who was impressed by the young man's enthusiasm for education. She encouraged him to visit Arizona State Teachers College (ASTC) and even called the college officials to help him out. He was soon not only enrolled, but he was also offered an on-campus job to help cover his expenses. This is noteworthy, because with his admission to the college, he became ASTC's first black student.

Riles graduated from ASTC in 1940 with a degree in education. During his college years, he supported himself, not only by working his on-campus job, but also by washing cars and hosting a radio jazz program in which he called himself "Dr. Rhythm." During his time in Flagstaff, he also worked at the Southwest Lumber Mill, where he served as a union secretary. After graduating, he moved to McNary, Arizona, to teach. There, he met his future wife, a teacher named Mary Louise Phillips. When Wilson left to fight in World War II as a pilot, Mary took a job at Flagstaff's Dunbar School. After the war, Wilson came back to Flagstaff and also became a teacher at Dunbar. In 1946, he was named principal, and he held that post until the school closed in 1954. In his spare time, Wilson pursued his master's degree, which he earned in 1947 at ASTC.

Wilson and Louise Riles made important contributions to education and were active in the community. They worked toward desegregation of not only the school system but also of local restaurants and other public establishments. Because they were respected in the community, others followed their lead in working toward these social changes. Thanks to all of these efforts, and to a growing national sentiment to desegregate schools, the Flagstaff School Board voted to desegregate in 1954. Most of the younger students went to South Beaver School, and the older ones went to Flagstaff Junior High, so Dunbar School was closed. This was a significant act by the school board, because it happened well before desegregation was required at the national level. Flagstaff was then looked on as a model for others to follow.

Wilson and Louise Riles in a classroom with six other adults, and possibly a teacher. *Northern Arizona University, Cline Library, Wilson and Louis Riles Collection.*

The Dunbar School was sold to a private company before it was purchased by the City of Flagstaff. In the 1960s, a new structure was laid over the original building. This resulted in what later came to be known as the Murdoch Center, which was named in honor of Cleo Murdoch, who had taught at the school longer than anyone else.

The Rileses later moved to California, where Wilson had an impressive career working in the State Department of Education. He became California's first black professional employee and was the first black person to be elected to an executive position in the California state government. Wilson served for a dozen years as State Superintendent of Public Instruction, and in 1976, Northern Arizona University (NAU) awarded him an honorary Doctor of Laws degree, which was only one of more than a half dozen honorary degrees awarded to him from various universities. In 1986, Building 15 at NAU, originally a gymnasium with a swimming pool, was remodeled into offices and classrooms and renamed Riles Hall.

Riles died in 1999, but his important work in civil rights and education and his contributions to the development of Flagstaff remain his lasting legacy.

PHILIP JOHNSTON

*I*n the "Seniors 1915" edition of *The Pine*—the student-published, semimonthly periodical from the Northern Arizona Normal School—a particular graduating senior is identified as the class poet who planned to move to Pasadena to continue his schooling. Philip Johnston had his whole life ahead of him, and though his name may not be immediately recognizable, his impact on history extends from the local hospitality industry of the 1930s to the international battlegrounds of World War II.

Philip Johnston was born September 17, 1892, in Topeka, Kansas. His parents were William and Margaret, and according to a 1910 census, the family would grow to include two younger siblings, David and Maud. William was a missionary, and in 1896, he moved his family to the western part of the Navajo Reservation to work with the tribe. As a reward for helping to settle a livestock rustling feud, he was granted permission to build a mission a dozen miles north of Leupp. It was here that Philip grew up mastering the Navajo language. In 1901, he accompanied his father and Navajo leaders to Washington, D.C., where Philip acted as translator between Theodore Roosevelt and the Navajos as they asked the president to add more land to the reservation. During World War I, Johnston went to France as a member of the United States Army's 319th Engineers. After the war ended, he attended graduate school at the University of Southern California, where he earned an engineering degree in 1925. After that, he worked as a civil engineer in Los Angeles while maintaining his ties to northern Arizona.

The year after Johnston graduated, the United States Numbered Highway System was established, which created an integrated organization of roads and highways that made travel across the country much more convenient. One of the first highways developed within this network was U.S. Route 66, which ran from Chicago to Santa Monica, California, and passed through Missouri, Kansas, Oklahoma, Texas, New Mexico and Arizona. This fabled highway, often referred to as the Mother Road, went through Flagstaff and brought an influx of tourists and other travelers to town. An outgrowth of this increased travel was the creation of motor hotels, also known as motorists' hotels. Later, the two words were combined to form the term *motels*. The first motels tended to be on the outskirts of towns and were run as mom-and-pop facilities. This was also the case in Flagstaff. By the mid-1930s Johnston became interested in this burgeoning motor hotel industry, and in 1936, he hired a contractor to build a motel three miles east of downtown Flagstaff. Johnston named it the El Pueblo Motor Court, and for years, it was one of the first visitor facilities for travelers arriving in Flagstaff from the east.

Located at 3120 East Route 66, the El Pueblo followed the fortunes of Route 66 and thrived for several decades. However, both of their futures began to dim in 1956, when the Federal Highway Act was passed and resulted in the creation of the Interstate Highway System. These new, high-speed highways often bypassed or replaced the older roadways, and such was the fate of Route 66, which was officially removed from the U.S. Highway System in 1985. Business at the El Pueblo accordingly declined, but it remained in operation. In the motel's later years, different groups and individuals talked about preserving the property because of its historic significance. Flagstaff Historic Preservation Officer Karl Eberhard summed up the reasons for preservation in a 2017 report:

> *The property itself is eligible for listing on the National Register of Historic Places as a national landmark. This property is notable because it is one of the oldest remaining motels in Flagstaff, it exemplifies the motor court building type, it is an example of an architectural style not normally found in Flagstaff, and it is associated with an individual [Johnston] who made significant contributions to American (and world) history.*[22]

The contributions to history that were mentioned by Eberhard were made by Johnston during World War II. After the Japanese attack on Pearl Harbor, Johnston remembered reading an article about how the military had used the Comanche language to transmit coded messages during maneuvers in Louisiana. He realized that the Navajo language could be used in the same way, and maybe even more effectively. Navajo was still only a spoken language (not written), and its use was restricted to the American Southwest. It incorporated a unique combination of syntax and tones that made it difficult for non-Navajos to understand. Johnston recruited four Navajos to demonstrate the validity of such an enterprise to the United States Marine Corps, and the Navajo Code Talker program was born.

The beauty of the Navajo Code was that it consisted of more than simple translations of English words into Navajo. First, the original twenty-nine Navajo men tasked with being code talkers created a list of Navajo words that each represented a letter of the English alphabet. *Dzeh*, for instance, is the Navajo word for "elk," so it represented the letter "e;" *moasi* is Navajo for "cat" and represented the letter "c," and so on. The code talkers realized that spelling out every single word this way could be time consuming, so they also developed words for military terms. For example, they used the Navajo word *atsá*, meaning "eagle," to refer to transport planes and *ca-lo*, meaning "shark," for destroyer ships. They developed a codebook to help other code

Technical Sergeant Philip Johnston on a recruiting tour of the Navajo Indian Reservation in 1942. *Northern Arizona University, Cline Library, Philip Johnston Collection.*

Navajo Code Talkers Henry Blake and George Kirk at the Battle of Bougainville in 1943. *United States Marine Corps.*

talkers learn the terms, but these were never taken into battle lest they fell into the hands of the enemy; all terms had to be memorized.

More than four hundred Navajos ultimately served as code talkers, and many of them were recruited by Johnston. They were deployed in the southwest Pacific Ocean, or the "Pacific Theater," during World War II, and they were also active in later military actions such as the Korean War. The program ended during the Vietnam War but not before saving probably thousands of lives. The Navajo Code remains the only spoken military code to have never been broken by an enemy.

Philip Johnston died in 1978, but his name will be forever remembered for his important role in the history of Arizona and beyond.

THE WONDERFUL WORLD OF DISNEY

*T*he *Wonderful World of Disney* is the second-longest-running primetime television program in America; it started in the mid-1950s as *Disneyland* and continued under various titles to the present. Through the years, the show has featured animated and live-action programming and has boasted a guest list that includes a longtime Flagstaff resident.

On October 27, 1954, *Disneyland* premiered on ABC, and was partly designed to advertise the Disneyland theme park, which opened on July 17, 1955. This was an important event in the history of entertainment, because it was the first television show produced by a major movie studio. Movie studios at the time were skeptical of television and thought that this expanding media would ruin the motion picture industry. With this new show, Walt Disney and his studio proved otherwise. The program also was effective in helping build support for the United States space program.

Each *Disneyland* episode focused on a different topic, which was often connected to one of the theme park's attractions. One of the most famous programs consisted of a five-part series that showcased "Frontierland" and featured Davy Crockett. Running from 1954 to 1955, this wildly popular serial spawned a countrywide Davy Crockett craze that saw children wearing coonskin caps and singing the show's theme song.

On the heels of this successful show, Disney began planning a "Tomorrowland" show in 1956, initially named *Man and Mars*. It would first introduce the universe as a topic and gradually narrow the discussion to Mars, highlighting the historical understanding of the planet, speculations about life and the possibilities of traveling there. To discuss the segment about travel to Mars, the studio contracted the services of rocket scientists Wernher von Braun—the German-born engineer and architect of the American space program—and Ernst Stuhlinger—von Braun's countryman and assistant in developing the rocket guidance and propulsion systems that were critical for manned spaceflight.

For general discussion about Mars, the studio contacted an institution that was long known for its research on Mars: Lowell Observatory. In a letter to the observatory director, Albert Wilson, that was dated March 13, 1956 (coincidentally, this would have been observatory founder and Mars specialist Percival Lowell's 101st birthday), producer and director, Ward Kimball, and assistant director, William Bosche, requested the observatory's assistance in creating the show. Kimball was a bit of a legend in the entertainment world by that time. He started working for Walt Disney in 1935 as an animator and came to be regarded as one of Disney's "Nine Old Men," the core group of animators that created many of the early Disney animated films. Kimball worked on *Snow White and the Seven Dwarfs*, *Pinocchio* (he created Jiminy Cricket), *Fantasia*, *Dumbo*, *Cinderella* and other classics.

Ward and Bosche wanted to come to Flagstaff and gather live footage of the facilities and staff at Lowell Observatory. They also requested that the observatory send one of its astronomers to travel to the Disney studio to narrate part of the show. On March 15, Wilson responded favorably and suggested that astronomer Earl ("E.C.") Slipher could fill the role of narrator. Within two weeks, Kimball sent Wilson a script and storyboard for the show, and he pointed out that the text was kept simple "so that the average viewer won't switch stations to 'Liberace' and his piano."

Slipher, who spent his entire professional career (1905–64) at Lowell Observatory, was widely recognized as one of the world's leading experts on Mars. He was also an active member of the Flagstaff community, serving on the Flagstaff City Council—including a stint as mayor from 1918 to 1920—and in the Arizona State Legislature. Slipher also regularly participated on a variety of local boards and committees focused on concerns from water and banking to the K-12 school system and college. He was a member of the committee that planned and raised money for a new community hotel (the Hotel Monte Vista, which opened in 1927) and served on Flagstaff's draft board during World War II.

E.C. Slipher observing Mars in South Africa in 1954. *Lowell Observatory Archives.*

Disney personnel traveled to the observatory in April to film the main segments of the show. The studio paid $1,350 in rental fees and costs to cover observatory staff salaries. In May, Slipher flew out to the Disney studios to film his narration piece. In writing about Slipher, Kimball noted, "Dr. Slipher did very well before the cameras. We put horn-rimmed glasses on him and everybody who has seen the footage comments that he looks like a typical astronomer."

The program was eventually called *Mars and Beyond* and was released as a theatrical featurette on December 4, 1957. It was narrated by voice actor Paul Frees, who is known for providing the voiceover and narration for a variety of Disney motion pictures, like *The Absent-Minded Professor*, and theme park attractions, like Pirates of the Caribbean. Frees was also well known for his character voice work that included Boris Badenov in the *Rocky and Bullwinkle* animated television series of the early 1960s and

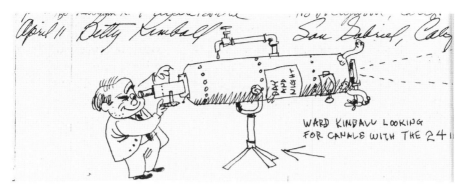

Drawing by Betty Kimball of her husband, Ward, looking through Lowell Observatory's twenty-four-inch Clark Telescope. *Lowell Observatory Archives.*

the Burgermeister Meisterburger in the 1970 stop-motion television classic *Santa Claus Is Comin' to Town.*

The opening scene of *Mars and Beyond* featured Walt Disney himself talking with a robot named GARCO. Following this, there was an introduction that outlined the early efforts to understand how the universe works, including the formation of our solar system and the possible development of life on other planets. This discussion soon moved to Mars, and the film included an eight-minute segment featuring Slipher. Fellow Lowell Observatory astronomers Vesto Melvin "V.M." Slipher and Henry Giclas also made short appearances. The film showed them operating the historic twenty-four-inch refracting telescope that the observatory's founder, Percival Lowell, had famously used decades earlier while formulating his controversial theories about life on Mars. V.M. was E.C.'s older brother, and he, like E.C., spent his entire professional career at Lowell Observatory. While he served as director for several decades, he is most remembered in scientific circles for being the first person to measure the so-called radial velocities of galaxies—essentially the first evidence of the expanding universe. Giclas was another longtime astronomer at Lowell who specialized in the study of comets and asteroids. He also led a decades-long survey that measured star positions. Both Giclas and his wife, Bernice, were active members of the Flagstaff community, and both of them were once recognized as the "Citizen of the Year."

After the Slipher and Lowell Observatory segment, the show considered possible means of traveling to and exploring Mars and concluded by imagining what life on the Red Planet might look like. The entire episode, which is officially season four, episode twelve of the *Disneyland* series, ran for fifty-three minutes. It proved popular with audiences and, two decades later, was edited to create an eighteen-minute educational film, *Cosmic Caper*s. In modern times, *Mars and Beyond* is considered a classic of television's golden age. It is still available to watch and serves as a portal back in time to when audiences around the country first experienced the mysteries of Mars.

Buffalo Park

*F*lagstaff is like many other rural communities, where residents often experience wildlife firsthand—families of deer graze near homes, raccoons clean themselves in the dog's water bowl and skunks waddle across yards while everyone holds their breath. But back in July 1969, residents were startled to run into buffalo and a multitude of other critters that are not normally seen walking around neighborhoods. The animals had escaped from Buffalo Park, Flagstaff's short-lived wildlife zoo that now serves as an outdoor recreation area for our two-legged species.

The story of Buffalo Park goes back to January 1963, when Flagstaff Chamber of Commerce President Jim Potter proposed a plan to create a wildlife park—similar to Yellowstone National Park—to the Flagstaff City Council. He proposed that the park would showcase buffalo, elk and other animals in a natural setting. He suggested that the park should be located on a city-owned tract of land atop McMillan Heights Mesa (that was later simplified to McMillan Mesa and is the same area where the United States Geological Survey would establish its primary facility in Flagstaff). The council approved the plan and agreed to a five-year lease of the land that included the construction of a road and the provision of water.

The Buffalo Park Committee was formed to oversee the development of the new park. Members of the committee included Potter, John G. Babbitt, Platt Cline and Rollin Wheeler—names that still resonate in this community. By July, the committee had raised $10,000, most of which was dedicated to building a seven-foot chain-link fence to surround the 217-acre park. This

Postcard of Buffalo Park. *Kevin Schindler's collection.*

fence and a stockade fence at the entrance were both in place by mid-January 1964, and various buildings were also being constructed.

The first animal in the park—a deer that had been trapped by National Park Service rangers in the Grand Canyon—arrived on January 31, 1964, and the first buffalo arrived on April 7. Eventually, the park boasted dozens of domesticated fauna and fowl, as well as more than two hundred wild animals, including elk brought in from Yellowstone National Park, antelope, ring-necked doves, Chinese and golden pheasants, Gambel's quails, wild ducks, Egyptian and Canadian geese, mouflon sheep, llamas, Barbary sheep, blackbuck antelope, Cornish game hens, peacocks, a javelina named Convair (named so because she had been flown in to Flagstaff on a Convair aircraft) and numerous barnyard animals.

Local artist Charles Bonney Jr., who was then a student at Arizona State College, offered to create a buffalo statue that would greet visitors at the park entrance. Bonney built a steel frame covered with wire mesh, which he then coated with a concrete and latex-silicon mixture. It weighed more three tons and was erected in the park on April 26, 1964. Bonney charged $500 for the statue, and the cost was covered by a donation from Carl Tremaine of Pacific Palisades, California.

On May 30, 1964, the park officially opened with an admission fee of one dollar per adult and fifty cents per child. The highlight attraction was a forty-five-minute tour of the grounds aboard one of the park's fleet, which included a pair of stagecoaches, two wagons, a mule train and a surrey that was donated by Flagstaff resident Fred Ball on behalf of his sister, actress Lucille Ball.

The tour featured sightings of buffalo, elk and other animals wandering in their natural habitats. It would start near the entrance to the park at the old-time stage depot, and from there, visitors would ride west and down into a canyon, around a bend and over a slight rise before stopping at the "Old Trapper's Cabin." There, they would hear legendary cowboy philosopher, radio star and raconteur O.T. Gillette spin a yarn or two. The tour would then proceed up a long rise to a mesa where Navajo women wove blankets in front of four hogans (traditional dwellings of the Navajo). Soon, the construction site of "Old Flagstaff"—an area that, when completed, would represent Flagstaff in the 1880s—would come into view, and this would be followed by the beginnings of "Fort Flag," a replica of a nineteenth-century frontier fort. From there, the tour would head back to the park entrance, where visitors could feed the smaller animals that were kept in cages made of split rail fencing. A June 26, 1964 commemorative insert in the *Arizona Daily Sun* captured the experience: "The sound of the past immediately tunes the visitor's ear to the 1880s as a Butterfield stage pulls up short at the newly completed replica of an old-time stage depot."

Postcard of O.T. Gillette in front of the "Old Trapper's Cabin" at Buffalo Park. *Kevin Schindler's collection.*

Buffalo Park guests at stagecoach driven by O.T. Gillette. *Arizona Historical Society, Flagstaff, Gladwell Richardson Collection.*

Modern view of the entrance to Buffalo Park featuring Charles Bonney's buffalo statue. *Kevin Schindler's collection.*

To ensure western authenticity, the park sought advice from a Warner Bros. film crew, which had been in Flagstaff filming *A Distant Trumpet*. The crew helped design many of the buildings and the rustic stockade fence. Warner Bros. even asked if they could use the park as a setting for future films, but this never happened.

Despite a successful first summer that saw some forty-seven thousand visitors, Buffalo Park soon ran into financial difficulties. The park hung on for several years but was finally doomed by the heavy snows of 1967 and 1968 and closed in 1969, though many of the animals remained on site for a while. The animals escaped on a number of occasions, including the time they made their way to the Sechrist School area to graze. A plan for Old Tucson Inc. to take over the park fell through, and in October 1969, the city ordered that all remaining animals be removed from the park.

In 1973, the Flagstaff City Council banned a proposed reroute of Highway 180 through the park and dedicated the site as a recreational area. The council later rescinded the ban, opening the possibility of paved roads running through the site. In 1986, Flagstaff residents voted to restore the ban to protect Buffalo Park from development.

Today, Bonney's statue and the stockade fence remain at the entrance to Buffalo Park, which is now a recreational area. Modern hiking trails follow the old stagecoach path, and walkers, runners and bikers can play where the buffalo once roamed.

ASTRONAUTS LAND IN FLAGSTAFF

*N*orthern Arizona is like a large, open-air geology classroom with a unique array of volcanic features as well as the world's best-preserved meteorite-impact crater and one of nature's most majestic displays, the Grand Canyon. Tourists from around the world flock to Flagstaff to embrace the area's beauty and wonder, but in 1963, voyagers on their way to another world came here to prepare for their missions.

This story traces back to May 25, 1961, when President John F. Kennedy boldly declared that the United States would send humans to the moon—and return them safely to Earth—before the end of the 1960s. To accomplish this, NASA would need to do a lot of things in a hurry, including bring on more astronauts to supplement the original Mercury 7 crew of Alan Shepard, John Glenn, Gus Grisson, Scott Carpenter, Wally Schirra, Gordon Cooper and Deke Slayton. On September 17, 1962, NASA announced the selection of a second group, a collection of nine pilots that became known variably as the New Nine, Next Nine and Nifty Nine. Their goal was to help develop the Gemini and Apollo programs, which were critical steps in meeting Kennedy's declaration. The group included Neil Armstrong, Frank Borman, Charles (Pete) Conrad, Jim Lovell, Jim McDivitt, Elliot See, Tom Stafford, Ed White and John Young. Of these men, all but Elliot See (who died in a plane crash) would fly in space. Of them, six would command missions to the moon, one would be the first American to walk in space and another would be the first person to walk on the moon.

While their work was initially focused on the engineering and technical aspects of getting to the moon, scientific components were soon added as a result of pressure put on NASA by scientists, like the geologist Eugene Shoemaker. Shoemaker thought that if humans were going to travel to another world, they should do more than just take a few steps, plant a flag and return home. He thought they should also make scientific observations and carry out experiments. To do this, the astronauts, who had strong engineering backgrounds but limited scientific experience, would need intense training to learn basic principles of observation, data collection and analysis. This training would help them become familiar with the geology, cartography and geography of the moon.

Shoemaker believed Flagstaff, with its rich geology that is analogous to that of the moon, would be an ideal location for much of this training. He even moved the United States Geological Survey's Branch of Astrogeology from Menlo Park, California, to Flagstaff to accomplish this. NASA agreed, and in early 1963, they planned to send the Next Nine to Flagstaff as a sort of trial run to evaluate the quality of training there. On January 9, 1963, the *Arizona Daily Sun* reported that Mercury heroes John Glenn and Scott Carpenter would accompany the Next Nine on a training session in northern Arizona the following week. Traveling from NASA's Manned Spaceflight Center (known today as the Johnson Space Center), the group planned to study geological features like Meteor Crater, which is a good analog to moon craters. While they were there, the astronauts would also learn about the lunar mapping efforts going on in Flagstaff.

At Lowell Observatory, the United States Air Force's Aeronautical Chart and Information Center (ACIC) rented the observatory's twenty-four-inch Clark Telescope to make geographic maps of the lunar surface. Observers would first identify lunar surface features, and artists armed with airbrushes would then render them into maps. Building on this effort, Flagstaff's newly established United States Geological Survey (USGS) Astrogeology Branch erected a new thirty-inch telescope on Anderson Mesa, southwest of town, to create lunar geological maps. Scientists used the ACIC maps as a base and added in geological features as observed through the new telescope.

On January 14, the proposed Flagstaff training session was in doubt due to snow in the area, which obscured much of the terrain that the astronauts were scheduled to study. The scheduling conflicts also meant that Glenn and Carpenter would not be able to make the trip. However, that afternoon, Charles Marshall of the USGS, who was in charge of the mapping efforts with the new thirty-inch telescope, surveyed the Flagstaff area and predicted that the snow would melt enough by the next day to allow training.

Flagstaff officials prepared to greet the astronauts the following morning, with Flagstaff Mayor Rollin Wheeler and Chamber of Commerce President James Potter leading the welcoming party. The astronauts would arrive via two airplanes landing at the Flagstaff Municipal Airport—they typically never traveled together so that the entire astronaut crew would not be wiped out in the event of an accident—which meant some of the astronauts arrived at 7:38 a.m. via Frontier Airlines, while others arrived at 7:42 a.m. riding a Bonanza Airlines flight.

The morning of Wednesday, January 16, dawned very cold, and when about forty Flagstaff dignitaries and scientists met the astronauts at the airport, the mercury read negative five degrees. Wheeler formally declared January 16 as "Space Age Day" in Flagstaff and welcomed the astronauts, as well as the half-dozen NASA officials who accompanied them. After about twenty minutes of introductions and hand shaking, the visitors drove to their hotel rooms at the Sentry Hiway House, located at the northeast corner of Route 66 and Fourth Street (in later years this was run as a Travelodge, but it was eventually torn down to make way for a Walgreens). Here, the astronauts changed out of their business suits and into weather-appropriate thermal underwear and training clothes.

Loading up into a fleet of gray government vehicles, the group headed out to Meteor Crater at 9:30 a.m. and met USGS geologists Gene Shoemaker and Charles Marshall, who taught the astronauts about the best-preserved impact crater in the world. The group then ate lunch before traveling over to Sunset Crater, where Monument Superintendent Russell Maham, Ranger Don Morris and Geologist Bill Breed of the Museum of Northern Arizona taught the astronauts about the geology of volcanic features.

After this daytime training, Lowell Observatory Director John Hall hosted dinner for the entourage at his recently built observatory home. The astronauts, trainers and other dignitaries enjoyed a buffet dinner prepared by Hall's wife, Ruth. Years later, Lowell Observatory Astronomer Henry Giclas recalled the event:

> Even though before-dinner libations were served, things started out rather stiffly with all the NASA brass on their good behavior. Then Bernice (Henry's wife) made some smart remark about the only experience she knew about exploring the moon was when the cow jumped over it, which cracked everybody up, and the party took on a much more relaxed and informal mood.[23]

Gene Shoemaker (lower left) teaching Apollo astronauts geology at Meteor Crater. This picture was taken during one of the astronauts' visits to northern Arizona subsequent to the 1963 visit. *Astrogeology Science Center, United States Geological Survey.*

After dinner, the group headed over to Lowell Observatory's ACIC office. For the next hour, scientists briefed the astronauts on lunar geography and geology, as well as the ACIC's mapping efforts of the moon and Mars. Some of the participating officials included Lowell Observatory Director Hall, Lowell Observatory's ACIC Office Head Bill Cannell, retired Lowell Observatory Astronomer E.C. Slipher, ACIC Artist Patricia Bridges, Gene Shoemaker and James Smith of ACIC's St. Louis office.

At midnight, the contingent broke up into three groups for telescope viewing. See, White and McDivitt stayed at Lowell to use its Clark twenty-four-inch telescope. Borman, Stafford and Armstrong, who ended up being the commanders of the first three manned missions to the moon, went to Arizona State College to use its twenty-four-inch reflector. The navy men, Lovell, Conrad and Young, headed to the U.S. Naval Observatory Flagstaff Station to use its forty-inch reflector.

Illustrator Patricia Bridges *(right)* briefs astronaut Pete Conrad on moon mapping at Lowell Observatory, 1963. *Lowell Observatory Archives.*

A note written by astronaut Neil Armstrong in E.C. Slipher's autograph book during his 1963 visit to Lowell Observatory. *Lowell Observatory Archives.*

The observers saw Mars and the moon, among other celestial objects. In viewing the moon, they compared lunar features with the terrestrial ones they had seen in the field at Meteor Crater and Sunset Crater. Henry Giclas, who was on hand at Lowell Observatory's Clark Telescope, recalled one of the astronauts remarking, "And this is where we are going," as he viewed the moon.[24] Some of the astronauts finished telescope viewing by 2:30 a.m., while others did not finish until 3:30 a.m. Once they were done, the astronauts went back to their rooms and slept for four hours. As Conrad commented: "One thing you can say for the space program, it has invented the twenty-six-hour day."[25]

In the morning, the astronauts headed over to Arizona State College for classroom geology and geography training by Shoemaker and the college's astronomer, Art Adel. After this briefing, six of the astronauts were taken to the airport, where, at the request of the Flagstaff Chamber of Commerce, they each left their handprints in cake cans filled with cement (the USGS Flagstaff office retains possession of these mementos.) Several Flagstaff dignitaries, including Chamber President Potter, Councilman Peter Lindemann and public works Director Art Kennedy, bid the astronauts farewell before the spacemen flew back to Houston aboard the noon Frontier Airlines flight.

The other three astronauts stayed in Flagstaff for several more hours to ski and talk with students. At 11:50 a.m., just before their colleagues flew out of Flagstaff, Borman, Lovell and Conrad visited Flagstaff High School and were greeted by Mayor Wheeler and School Superintendent Wilfred Killip. The astronauts then talked for about thirty minutes to 1,900 junior and senior high students and teachers who had gathered in the gym. The students madly cheered for each astronaut, and two young ladies even fainted when Borman was introduced.

Half an hour later, the trio went to City Hall to make their own handprints before eating lunch at The Gables Restaurant, which was located at the intersection of Milton Road and Route 66 and later run as Lu Mandarin Buffet. Then Lovell, who wanted to learn more about Sunset Crater geology, headed back to the crater with Gene Shoemaker before joining the others and going to Arizona Snowbowl with Potter and past Chamber president Paul Weaver. They didn't have a chance to ski, but they did ride up the new chairlift on Agassiz Peak and enjoyed a grand view of the surrounding cinder cone–splattered landscape. They spent more than an hour at Snowbowl before heading back to town.

That night, at about seven o'clock, the astronauts went to Arizona State College and spoke to about nine hundred students and local residents at the Student Union auditorium. They then answered questions for about fifteen minutes, shook hands with College President J. Lawrence Walkup and left for the airport, where Mayor Wheeler, Potter and City Clerk Harry Field bid them adieu prior to their eight o'clock Frontier flight back to Houston.

The trip proved successful, and through the ensuing years, Flagstaff would again welcome the Next Nine and other astronauts to Flagstaff for in-depth geology training, instrument testing and other training necessary to fly to the moon. In fact, every astronaut who went to the moon trained in Flagstaff, and modern NASA astronauts continue to come to the area to prepare for future missions into space.

MR. FLAGSTAFF

$\mathcal{M}$any of the details in this book come from the pages of Flagstaff's newspaper, which was originally a weekly, known as the *Coconino Sun*. Established in 1883, it was converted to a daily newspaper in 1946, and the name was changed to the *Arizona Daily Sun*. For years, this paper was published by Platt Cline, so it seems poetic to end this book with an introduction to him.

Platt Cline was a man of immense energy and wide-ranging intellect. He used his clout as editor of the *Arizona Daily Sun* to champion the creation of Northern Arizona University (NAU), desegregate Flagstaff and foster better relations with Native American tribes.

Platt Herrick Cline was born on February 7, 1911, in Mancos, Colorado, to Gilbert Timothy Cline and Jessie Hatfield Baker. He graduated from Mancos High School in 1928 and from the New Mexico Military Institute in 1930, which is where he began his journalism career on the institute's yearbook staff. Cline attended the University of Colorado at Boulder for one year before returning to Mancos, where he was a reporter for the *Mancos Times-Tribune*. He married Barbara Decker in 1936, and in 1937, they moved to Norwood, Colorado, where they published the weekly *Post-Independent*. They moved to Flagstaff in 1938, and Platt went to work for the *Coconino Sun*, the *Winslow Mail* and, during the war years, the *Tribune-News* in Holbrook as managing editor. He returned to Flagstaff in 1945 and was the editor when the *Arizona Daily Sun* was launched on August 5, 1946. He became publisher in 1952 and president in 1966 before retiring in 1976. During his thirty-year tenure at the *Daily Sun*, Flagstaff's population mushroomed from about five thousand to thirty thousand people.

Cline claimed he was the first to come up with the idea of converting Arizona State College to university status, but he clearly credited then-president J. Lawrence Walkup with getting the job done by skillfully courting the state legislature. NAU was officially launched on May 1, 1966, and the first recipient of an honorary doctorate was none other than Platt Cline. Cline, through his relationship with NAU and his position at the *Arizona Daily Sun*, was a strong and very effective proponent of good "town and gown" relations. Cline has been described as the unofficial advisor to three NAU presidents: Lawrence Walkup, Eugene Hughes and Clara Lovett, and he was well regarded in that capacity.

Cline and his wife, Barbara's, contributions to NAU are too numerous to relate, and they include the establishment of ten different funds, most of which were dedicated to his first love: the NAU Library. In 1988, NAU named its newly constructed library the Cline Library in honor of Platt and Barbara. In 1984, Platt instituted a fund known as the Cline Fund for the Humanities, which enabled the creation of the university's first speaker's series, which ultimately led to visits by such distinguished personages as Nobel Laureates Francis Crick and Herbert Simon, Pulitzer Prize–winning author Larry McMurty, Chairman of the National Endowment for the Humanities Lynne Cheney and Principal Chief Wilma Mankiller of the Cherokee Nation to make presentations on campus.

Eugene Hughes, who was the president of NAU from 1979 to 1993, credits Cline with helping NAU build a strong relationship with the Native American tribes in the area. Hughes said he was particularly impressed by Cline's fascination and relationship with the Hopi and that it "rubbed off" on him, prompting him and other school officials to pursue more initiatives to serve Native Americans. Hughes has a lasting memory of Cline's resourcefulness in his president emeritus's office in NAU's Old Main building; Cline managed to track down and purchase the original desk, which was built around 1895 and used by the principal of the campus when it was still the Arizona Normal School, and he had it delivered from Sedona to Flagstaff, where it remains to this day.

In 1954, soon after the decision in *Brown v. Board of Education* but well before the Civil Rights Act of 1964, blacks were still segregated in Dunbar School on the south side of town. Cline and Wilson Riles decided to do something about it. As the story goes, they went store-to-store, telling everyone that, as of a certain date, everybody would open and welcome

Left: Platt Cline. *Kevin Schindler's collection.*

Below: Modern view of Cline Library. *Kevin Schindler's collection.*

black people. Because of the reputation and persistence of both men, it worked. In a related incident, Cline took Riles to the local theater and both men sat in the "white" section. Given Cline's enormous reputation, not a word was said to either man, so the theater was thus integrated.

There is another interesting story, related by Mike Patrick, who was managing editor of the *Arizona Daily Sun* in the late 1980s and early 1990s, that sheds light on the kind of person Platt Cline was. He remembers a day when Cline, who was by then retired, came into the newsroom while a new reporter was typing:

> *He was wearing what he always wore: gray slacks with protruding threads here and there, a well-worn, long-sleeved blue cotton shirt and old, comfortable shoes. The reporter waved him over. I saw her lips moving and Platt's head nodding in reply. He bent down, picked up something and left the newsroom. I thought it odd but went back to work. I bumped into Platt later and asked what the exchange was all about. Platt smiled. "Your new reporter thought I was the janitor," he said, "so of course, I emptied her trash."*[26]

These accomplishments, which only begin to scratch the surface of Cline's many causes, make him one of the community's most important citizens, and they earned him the well-deserved sobriquet of "Mr. Flagstaff."

Notes

Henry Fountain Ashurst

1. Johnson, *Arizona Politicians*, 114.
2. Ibid., 115.
3. Ibid.
4. Ibid., 113.
5. Ibid.

The 1894 Lowell Expedition

6. Lowell, *Mars and Its Canals*, 6.

A Giant Pockmark on the Earth

7. Lindbergh, *Spirit of St. Louis*, 360.

Clyde Tombaugh Discovers Pluto

8. Tombaugh and Moore, *Out of the Darkness*, 25.
9. Letters and telegrams in Lowell Observatory archives.

A Grand Bicycle Race

10. *Coconino Sun* (Flagstaff, AZ).
11. *Coconino Sun*.

The Weatherford Hotel

12. *Coconino Sun*, "Weatherford Dining Rooms to Be Opened Tomorrow, December 24—An Elegant Menu," December 23, 1899.

Leave It as It Is

13. "President Passes Through Flagstaff," *Coconino Sun*, May 9, 1903.
14. Ibid.

Lake Mary

15. Timothy Riordan, Letter to T.E. McCullough, RMSHP archives, December 31, 1932.

Grand Falls

16. Sitgreaves, *Report of an Expedition*, 8.

The Orpheum Theatre

17. Joe Meehan, interview by Kevin Schindler, 2005.

18. "New Orpheum Theatre Will Open Next Thursday," *Coconino Sun*, August 25, 1916.
19. Chris Scully, interview by Kevin Schindler, 2017.

The Hotel Monte Vista

20. *Coconino Sun*.

Weatherford Road

21. The Coconino County Board of Supervisors to the Secretary of the Department of Agriculture (April 17, 1916).

Philip Johnston

22. "Karl Eberhard, Karl," El Pueblo Motor Inn website, accessed December 18, 2017, www.elpueblomotorinn.blogspot.com.

Astronauts Land in Flagstaff

23. Giclas, "Personal Reminiscences" (undated manuscript in Lowell Observatory Archives).
24. Ibid.
25. Paul Sweitzer, "Astronauts Prove Big Hit Thursday in Talks to Flagstaff Hi School Students," *Arizona Daily Sun*, January 18, 1963.

Mr. Flagstaff

26. Eugene Hughes, interview by Mike Kitt, 2018.

FURTHER READING

*M*uch of the information in this book was gleaned from old issues of the *Arizona Daily Sun* newspaper and its predecessor, the *Coconino Sun*. In addition, the following have also been useful:

Aaseng, Nathan. *Navajo Code Talkers*. New York: Walker and Company, 1992.

Ashurst, Henry Fountain. *A Many-Colored Toga: The Diary of Henry Fountain Ashurst*. Tucson: University of Arizona Press, 1962.

Babbitt, James E. "The Impassable Dream: John W. Weatherford's San Francisco Mountain Boulevard." *The Journal of Arizona History* 47, no. 2 (2006).

Babbitt, James E., and John G. DeGroff III. *Flagstaff (Images of America)*. Charleston, SC: Arcadia Publishing, 2009.

Brundage-Baker, Joan. "The Lakes Mary." *Arizona Capitol Times*, August 25, 2014.

Cline, Platt. *Mountain Town: Flagstaff's First Century*. Flagstaff, AZ: Northland Press. 1994.

———. *They Came to the Mountain*. Flagstaff: Northern Arizona University with Northland Press, 1976.

Coconino County Board of Supervisors to the Secretary of the Department of Agriculture. Cline Library Special Collections, April 17, 1916.

Colton, Harold S., and Frank C. Baxter. *Days in the Painted Desert and the San Francisco Mountains: A Guide*. Flagstaff, AZ: Coyote Range, 1927.

DeGroff, John G., III. *Flagstaff (Postcard History Series)*. Charleston, SC: Arcadia Publishing, 2011.

Duffield, Wendell. *Volcanoes of Northern Arizona*. Grand Canyon, AZ: Grand Canyon Association, 1997.

Eberhard, Karl. The El Pueblo Motor Inn's website, www.elpueblomotorinn.blogspot.com, December 18, 2017.

Farretta, Kathleen. "Progressive Era Community-Builders: The Riordan Brothers of Flagstaff, Arizona Territory, 1884–1904." M.A. thesis, Northern Arizona University, 2004.

Giclas, Henry, "Personal Reminiscences." Lowell Observatory Archives.

Grey, Zane. *The Call of the Canyon*. New York: Grosset and Dunlap, 1924.

Hochderffer, George. *Flagstaff Whoa! The Autobiography of a Western Pioneer*. Flagstaff: Northern Arizona University, 1965.

Hoyt, William Graves. *Planets X and Pluto*. Tucson: University of Arizona Press, 1980.

Hughes, Eugene. Personal communication with Mike Kitt, 2018.

Jackson, Marie D. *Stone Landmarks: Flagstaff's Geology and Historic Building Stones*. N.p.: Piedra Azul Press, 1999.

Johnson, James W. *Arizona Politicians: The Novel and the Notorious*. Tucson: University of Arizona Press, 2002.

Lindbergh, Charles. *The Spirit of St. Louis*. New York: Charles Scribner's Sons, 1953.

Lowell, Percival. *Mars and Its Canals*. New York: MacMillan, 1906.

Mangum, Richard, and Sherry Mangum. *Flagstaff Past and Present*. Flagstaff, AZ: Northland Publishing, 2003.

Meehan, Joe. Personal communication with Kevin Schindler, 2005.

Olberding, Susan Deaver. *Fort Valley Then and Now: A Look at an Arizona Settlement*. Flagstaff, AZ: Fort Valley Publishing, 2002.

Riordan, Timothy, to T.E. McCullough, Riordan Mansion State Historic Park archives, December 31, 1932.

Rowland, Ann T. "Henry Fountain Ashurst: The Silver-Tongued Sunbeam of the Painted Desert." *The Smoke Signal*, no. 91 (2012).

Schindler, Kevin. *The Far End of the Journey: Lowell Observatory's 24-inch Clark Telescope*. Lowell Observatory, 2015.

Schindler, Kevin, and Bonnie Stevens. *Flagstaff Festival of Science: The First 25 Years*. Flagstaff: Flagstaff Festival of Science, 2014.

Schindler, Kevin, and Will Grundy. *Pluto and Lowell Observatory: A History of Discovery at Flagstaff*. Charleston, SC: The History Press, 2018.

Schindler, Kevin, and William Sheehan. *Northern Arizona Space Training.* Charleston, SC: Arcadia Publishing, 2017.

Scully, Chris. Personal communication with Kevin Schindler, 2017.

Sitgreaves, Lorenzo. *Report of an Expedition Down the Zuni and Colorado Rivers.* Washington, D.C.: Robert Armstrong, 1853.

Smith, Dean. *Brothers Five: The Babbitts of Arizona.* Tempe: Arizona Historical Foundation, 1989.

Tombaugh, Clyde, and Patrick Moore. *Out of the Darkness: The Planet Pluto.* Mechanicsburg, PA: Stackpole Books, 1980.

Vecchio, Janolyn G. Lo. "Owned and Operated by a Woman: Mary Costigan and Flagstaff's First Radio Station." *The Journal of Arizona History* 59, no. 1 (2018).

Wallace, Andrew. "Across Arizona to the Big Colorado: The Sitgreaves Expedition of 1851." *Journal of the Southwest* 26, no. 4 (1984).

Wilcox, David. "The Museum of Northern Arizona, 1928–2008." *Journal of the Southwest* 52, no. 4 (2010).

ABOUT THE AUTHORS

*K*evin Schindler is a native of Ohio, but he has lived in Flagstaff for more than twenty years and worked at Lowell Observatory for most of that time. He's always been interested in history, from the very old of the cosmos and ancient of fossils to the comparatively modern scientists and their research. He graduated from Marietta College (Ohio) in 1987 with a degree in geology and a strong focus in paleontology. He currently serves as the Lowell Observatory's historian after two decades of leading the observatory's education and outreach efforts. Schindler is an active member of Flagstaff's history and science communities, having served as sheriff of the Flagstaff Corral of Westerners International for thirteen years and as a board member of the Flagstaff Festival of Science for a similar length of time. When he is not digging through the Lowell Observatory's archives, he is writing articles for a variety of publications and contributing to a bi-weekly astronomy column, "View from Mars Hill," for the *Arizona Daily Sun* newspaper. This is his sixth book.

*M*ichael Kitt has had a strong interest in writing since his college days and has authored more than one hundred articles and technical papers, in addition to one book. He graduated from the City

University of New York with a bachelor's degree in chemistry and a master's degree in business administration. While in the U.S. Army, he developed and edited an internal newsletter called *Resonance* on behalf of the Rock Island Arsenal research facility. During his thirty-year career with Pfizer, he wrote many technical papers devoted to pharmaceutical manufacturing and quality control. He also contributed articles to the company's employee
newspaper. He is a popularizer of lunar observing, having contributed over forty articles and columns to such publications as *Astronomy Magazine, The Observer's Guide* and *Selenology*. He authored the book *The Moon: An Observing Guide for Backyard Telescopes*, which remained in print for more than a decade and was translated into French for sale in Canada. More recently, he has been a contributor to the Lowell Observatory's newsletter, *The Lowell Observer*, and an editorial assistant for the Museum of Northern Arizona's periodic publication, *Plateau*. Now retired, he serves on a variety of nonprofit boards.